About the Authors

Don Fried lived all over Europe for 30 years, working in Information Technology services. He returned to the U.S. in 2004 and retired from the business world in 2006 to try his hand at writing. Five of Don's plays were produced during 2007 and 2008, and another two are scheduled for production in 2009. *Ups and Downs* is his first book. During their trek in the Alps, Don and David outlined a psychological thriller that they keep telling each other they'll get around to starting.

Don lives in Niwot, Colorado, near Boulder, with his wife, Rhonda (whenever she's not in Austin, Texas with their grandchildren). Look at Don's website, www.don.fried.cc, for news of his writing activities and upcoming productions of his plays.

David Kassin Fried was born in the Netherlands, thanks to his parents having lived all over Europe for 30 years. Though he was raised primarily in England, he moved to Austin, Texas in 1999 to attend college and has lived there ever since.

David was a child actor, co-starring in the London premiere of *Conversations with My Father*, starring Judd Hirsch. Since returning to the U.S. he's worked as a writer, actor, and director, and in 2005 started his own writing and editing company, which delivers technical documentation, marketing communications, and outstanding works of literature like the one you're about to read.

Ups & Downs is David's first book, too. He lives in Austin with his wife, Angela, whom you'll meet in a few pages. Check out David's website at www.dkfwriting.com.

UPS & DOWNS

The (Mis)Adventures of a Crusty Old Fart and His Bouncy Son as They Trek Through the Alps

---

DON FRIED & DAVID KASSIN FRIED

Illustrated by Simon Matthews

Published by DaDo Publishing, PO Box 9065, Austin, TX 78766, USA.

First printed, 2009, by DaDo Publishing.

Maps by Donald R. Fried. Fridli diagram on page 40 by David Kassin Fried. Handwritten notes on page 120 by Donald R. Fried. Photograph in Epilogue by Jen White, © Angela Kieke Fried & David Kassin Fried. All other photographs by Angela Kieke Fried, David Kassin Fried, and Donald R. Fried. Cartoons by Simon Matthews, © 2008 David Kassin Fried and Donald R. Fried. "Wherever I May Roam" lyrics on page 57 © James Alan Hetfield and Lars Ulrich, reprinted by permission of Creeping Death Music. Bible quote on pages 73 and 188 from Numbers 32:13.

ISBN: 1-4392-1483-2

Thanks to all the people who helped us at every step of the way in getting this book published, and our apologies for not mentioning everyone by name. Special thanks to Rhonda Fried, Eric Fried, Angela Fried, Craig Wesley Divino, Bob Fried and Elizabeth Peltier O'Connor for editing help; Audrey Kruger and Amber Burke for help with our website; Patrick Cheffins, Ian Dundas, Elena and Tomas for their hospitality in London and Zurich; and all the people who made this trip such an extraordinary adventure. (And for the people who were nasty to us along the way, screw you.)

In the summer of 2002, Don and his father-in-law, Richard Kassin (along with their support crew, their respective wives), walked and pedaled from Lands End to John O'Groats – the southwest tip of Cornwall to the northeast tip of Scotland. They traveled a total of 1,068 miles, comprising 811 miles walking and 257 miles of cycling, and it took them 60 days. Richard celebrated his 74th birthday on the trail.

On May 7, 2005, Richard was diagnosed with mesothelioma, the cancer associated with asbestos exposure. He was given 6 months to live. But Richard never liked being told what to do, and lived life to the fullest for another 3 years before passing away on June 27, 2008.

When we began this journey it was with him in our hearts, and when we wrote this book it was, in part, so he could experience the trip vicariously. This book is dedicated to Richard Kassin, a man whose life certainly had its ups and downs.

Donald & David Fried
September 2008

Via Alpina Trails

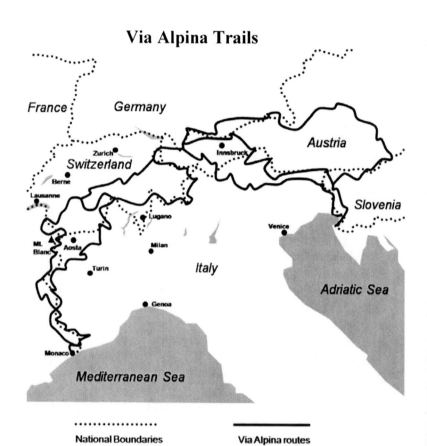

France
Germany
Austria
Switzerland
Zurich
Innsbruck
Berne
Slovenia
Lausanne
Lugano
Venice
Mt. Blanc
Aosta
Milan
Italy
Turin
Adriatic Sea
Genoa
Monaco
Mediterranean Sea

·················
National Boundaries

──────────
Via Alpina routes

Prologue

This whole thing started in the spring of 2006. David and Angela had just started dating, and a friend of theirs was moving to New Zealand. David asked Angela, "If I wanted to walk across New Zealand, would you come with me?" to which her response was, "In a second." They set June 2007 as the date for the trip, and David called his father, Don, to invite him to come along. Don's response: "You know, it's winter there in June." Oops. Forgot about that.

Over the course of the next week the three did some research and discovered the Via Alpina (www.via-alpina.com), a set of trails that follows the high ground of the Alps through Switzerland, France, Italy, Austria, Germany, Slovenia and their smaller cousins, Monaco and Lichtenstein. Angela would come for the first 3 weeks, while Don (who's retired) and David (who's a freelance writer) would spend two full months hiking the routes through Switzerland, France, and Italy.

It should be noted that none of the three was especially prepared or qualified for such an undertaking. But we'll get to that.

Original Planned Route

National Boundaries

Doubt, Dither and Ditz

Don June 19th

While I waited in the British Airways lounge at JFK Airport in New York City and David trolled for things to eat (which is something he spends a substantial portion of his time doing), I tried to control my growing sense of panic. The past 10 days had been characterized by what I had started to refer to as the three "Ds": **doubt, dither** and **ditz**.

First, **doubt**. Was I absolutely out of my mind? Who was I kidding, thinking I could carry my clothes, shelter, food, cooking utensils, emergency gear and all the other things necessary to keep me alive and dry and warm while walking up and down mountains for 2 months? Why would I want to? I was nearly 56 years old, for crying out loud! And it's not as though I didn't know what I was getting into. Five years earlier my father-in-law, Richard, and I had walked the length of Great Britain "B&B-to-B&B" from the southwest tip of Cornwall to the northeast tip of Scotland – nearly 1,100 miles in 60 days. While I got in great shape and saw a lot of wonderful scenery and de-stressed more than I had for 30 years, I lost 25 pounds (which I didn't have to lose), and I did damage to my feet and knees from which I still hadn't recovered. I also spent the following 4 months hungry 24 hours a day – your body gets used to consuming 6,000 calories a day and wants to continue, whether you still need it or not. And did I mention the rain? That July was the third wettest in England's history, and that's really saying something. So I understood what this walk was likely to be. But I was doing it anyway. Sheesh!

As for **dither** – there are a thousand things to consider and plan and buy and pack for a trek like this. If you're on top of a mountain miles away from the nearest civilization and you realize that you've forgotten something fairly important like, say, your tent or the toilet paper, you're going to wish you'd planned and packed better. But since I'm retired and for the past 10 days I'd had nothing to do, I couldn't get myself excited about doing much. So I'd head off to my local camping store in Boulder, Colorado, to buy a box of waterproof matches. Then I'd come home. Then I'd go to Wal-Mart (which is next door to the camping store) to buy some pain killer tablets. Then I'd come home. Then I'd go back to the camping store to buy some camping soap. Then I'd come home. Of course, there was lots of time spent sitting and staring at the wall in between. And so it went for about 7 days. Then, in the last 3 days, I really got serious.

That's when I proceeded to **ditz**. Everything I touched disappeared. Things I was sure I had packed were nowhere to be found. I'd search my backpack three times, then turn the house over four times before I would find what was missing – usually in the first place I'd looked 3 hours earlier. Finally everything was packed and I resolved not to look at it or touch it until I left. But on the kitchen counter, I found a lens from a pair of eyeglasses. OK, I thought, it must have popped out of my spare pair of reading glasses as I was packing them. So I opened the backpack and looked for the glasses. They weren't there. I searched the entire house. Still nothing. Finally, on my camping supply shelf in the basement, which was the first place I'd looked after searching through the backpack, I found a plastic bag with the glasses. **And** my headlamp. **And** my soap. And my toothbrush and toothpaste and twenty other absolute essentials. If the lens hadn't popped out, I would've ended up on the trail the first night without much of what I needed. At that point I started getting really scared. If not for the fact that nearly the same thing had happened to me before starting the walk through Britain, I would've thought that I'd suddenly gone seriously senile. I hoped it was just nerves.

Some Things Never Change

David   June 20th-21st

Considering it sees more traffic than just about any other airport in the world, Heathrow has this uncanny ability to create headaches out of the most mundane tasks. Angela (my fiancée), Dad and I had decided to make a stop in Southeast England so that I could show Angela where I grew up and where I went to high school.

But we neglected to realize what a challenge it would be to escape from Heathrow Airport. After 3 days of chaos packing and moving out of my apartment;[1] waking up at 6 am to retrieve my passport (which I'd forgotten in a filing cabinet all the way at the back of my storage unit); a 3-hour flight from Austin to New York; a 5-hour layover at JFK; a transatlantic red-eye to London and the obligatory mile-and-a-half walk to Passport Control, we were now standing at baggage claim, waiting.

Waiting, waiting, waiting for our luggage to arrive. Such is life

---

[1] Actually, those last few days I and my cats were staying in my mother's Austin apartment. Mom hates cats, so the condition of their staying at her apartment for the final week was that they live in the bathroom the whole time. They were pretty pissed about that. It took them about 30 seconds to figure out how to open the door and escape, at which point they would shout "Freedom!!!" and run under the bed. They couldn't move under there, but I was unable to reach them, so they would stare at me with a look of immense satisfaction and disdain as I groped ineffectually in their direction. When I finally grabbed them and threw them back into the bathroom, I pitched a bench up against the door – which delayed their escape to about 45 seconds, leading to another hour of ineffectual groping. Eventually I figured out how to lock them in the bathroom, but I quickly learned that I should only open the door when (a) I was getting ready to feed them, or (b) I was willing to give them the run of the house for a few minutes ... before feeding them.

at Heathrow Airport.

The minutes passed – 15, 30, 45. Finally, an announcement came over the loudspeaker: "For passengers awaiting their bags on BA 116, we are locating your bags and they should be out in 10 minutes." About 20 minutes later, another announcement: "We've found your bags and they should be right out." About 10 minutes later, a third: "If passengers from Flight 116 will come to the service desk to fill out claim forms, we will endeavor to locate your bags and have them delivered to you some time today." So we and 200 other people trooped over to the service desk and waited about 10 minutes before the fourth and final announcement, informing us that they had located our bags, they were being loaded onto the carousel now, and we should get our asses back over there pronto. It was another half-hour before our bags came out.

Good to know that after 8 years out of the country, some things never change.

Next, rental car. At my suggestion, Dad had booked through a discount website, and though I've always had fabulous results in the past, this time the cheapest car rental company by about £12 ($24) per day was a company we'd never heard of. I've long since forgotten the name, so we'll just call it "Rentapeezoshit."

As per the instructions on Rentapeezoshit's confirmation sheet, we called a toll-free number to inquire about their "shuttle service." A nice man on the other end told Dad that there were two options for the shuttle service: we could either spend 45 minutes taking a train to another terminal and then go outside and pay £4 ($8) per person for a bus, or we could take a taxi directly from this terminal and pay £25.

As Dad shared this news with me and Angela, the three of us stared longingly outside the terminal. We watched the shuttle buses for Enterprise, Avis, and Hertz drive by, picking up and dropping off happy tourists. We thought about the £25 we were about to spend on the taxi, all so we could save £24 total on 2-days' car rental. Somehow, it just didn't seem worth it.

Then, when we finally got to Rentapeezoshit's lot, the car they gave us had almost no gas, which meant riding fumes to the nearest petrol station and filling up someone else's empty gas tank at what we're sure were the highest petrol prices in Southeast England.

Every time I come to England I make it a point of getting drunk with Dan, my former boss at the fish and chips shop. Though we wouldn't be able to party on this particular trip, I always enjoy walking into his shop and surprising him, so in we went. I asked the man behind the counter if Dan was there. He looked at the three of us suspiciously and asked why we were asking. I told him that I used to work for Dan about 10 years ago, to which he breathed a sigh of relief and said, "No, Dan went broke about a year and a half ago, sold the shop, and I haven't seen him since." Apparently he thought we were creditors, coming to take out Dan's kneecaps. I can understand how he would think we were hit men – I hadn't shaved in 3 days and looked like a mature 12-year-old, and Angela's pout can make a grown man weep (it's true – you don't want to test this one).

We ordered our fish and chips to go and took it to the Bekonscot Model Village, the oldest miniature village in the world and Beaconsfield's number one tourist attraction. When I was growing up, Bekonscot was Dad's favorite place in the whole wide world, and any time someone would come to visit us he would take them there, whether they wanted to go or not, and each time he would snicker at the names on the miniature storefronts (Sam & Ella's Butcher, Argue & Twist Solicitor, etc.) as though it were the first time he'd seen it.

It started raining just as we got there (good to know some things never change), so we took shelter in a little greenhouse with what seemed like 600 5-year-olds on a school outing. They were just finishing up their lunch, and we watched the comical chaos as their teachers pulled raincoats out of a big pile and shouted things like, "Gerald, why are you wearing your brother's coat? You look like a right plonker! Whose is this? It doesn't have a name in it! This is why I've been telling you since September to put your names in your coats. I'm *really cross* right now!!"

The children eventually got into their raincoats and filed out, and we took our seats at the table and ate our now soggy fish and chips.

It was going to be a long trip.

Bekonscot Model Village

East to West Across Switzerland

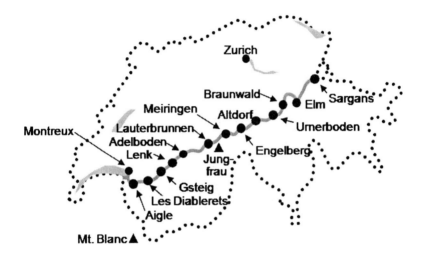

On the Road

By the time we got to baggage claim in Zurich, our suitcases were coming out on the carousel. Quite a difference from Heathrow, but as you'll see, pretty much everything in Switzerland is quite a bit different from the UK. Except, that is, for the prices (extortionately high) and the weather (alternating between overcast and raining). While heading to the airport train station, we passed a newspaper stand. The photographs on the front pages of all the local papers were of the torrential rainstorms of the past several days and the flooding they had caused. I thought back to my end-to-end walk across Britain. Nah, it couldn't happen again. ... Could it? ...

The Fried family left the United States in 1974, and lived all but four of the next 30 years overseas. Almost all of it was in Western Europe, and we had lived in Zurich from 1987 to 1989. We were now on our way to see Elena and Tomas, friends with whom we'd stayed in contact for the last 20 years. David was 6 years old when we moved to Zurich, and Elena immediately became his surrogate grandmother.

Elena is an enthusiastic fellow polyglot; as with many Swiss, she speaks German, French, Italian, and English, but she also speaks Czech and Japanese. She is always studying one or another language, and during our conversations she always has a pen and paper handy to write down unfamiliar words and expressions so that she can study them later. Elena is a matronly woman in her early 70s, but with the imperious, regal gaze familiar from statues and paintings of Queen Victoria. I have to admit that when I first met her, that stare gave me the willies. Even now, 20 years later, I subconsciously sit up straighter and pay more attention to what I'm saying whenever I'm around her.

Tomas was a professor of nuclear chemistry at Zurich University for his entire career; he retired about 10 years ago and continues to write academic papers that he presents at conferences around the world. He is a tall, erect, unassuming man of near 80, always wearing the signature tweed sports coat of the lifelong academic – even when he is outside doing the gardening. Much of the time he sits quietly observing and listening to the conversation with a shy smile on his face. Then, invariably, he will make a comment or ask a question that reveals that he has been absorbing and cataloging every word. And often, as you might expect from a nuclear chemist, what he says reveals that the man is absolutely brilliant.

Elena and Tomas were bemused and concerned with the plans for our trek. Being native Swiss, they are more enthusiastic and have far more experience with mountains than you would expect from lifelong city dwellers. But along with that experience comes a healthy respect for the dangers inherent in somebody of my age heading up to where the air is thin and the hair shouldn't be. As for the rain, well, it had been bad recently, but that wouldn't continue. (Would it?)

Elena fed us lunch and presented us each with a large bar of Lindt chocolate to sustain us on the trail. Then we transferred our gear from our suitcases to our backpacks, hoisted them onto our shoulders, and immediately toppled over onto our backs and began flailing around helplessly like turtles. It wasn't quite that bad, of course, but even though I'd done a "test lift" at home, the prospect of having to carry that weight through the mountains and live on the contents for the next 2 months was somehow much more intimidating now that it was imminent. And we hadn't bought food or propane gas canisters yet.

Like me, Tomas is a map freak. He has topographical maps of most of Switzerland, but they are all from the 1970s, which means that some of the trails will have changed. However, since these maps are expensive (24 CHF[2] – about $20 – each) and we would walk through each one in about a day and a half, we thought we'd save $1,000 and take our chances. So Tomas and I went through his collection and selected maps for the first 20 days. After that David, Angela and I would be returning to Zurich to bring Angela to the airport for her flight home, and we'd replenish our map supply.

We piled our backpacks into Elena's old Volvo station wagon, and she drove us to the main Zurich train station. We had decided to start the trek by walking across Switzerland from east to west, so our first destination was the small city of Sargans near the border with Liechtenstein. From Sargans it would be a 3-day walk up and over the Foopass and down to the small village of Elm.

The train ride was beautifully scenic, along the upper reaches of

---

[2] CHF, believe it or not, is the symbol for Swiss Francs. CH, which is the acronym on Swiss license plates, stands for Confederatio Helvetica. The Helvetii were the dominant tribe in the area when the Romans moved in around the 2nd century BC, and the name stuck.

the Rhein River and the south sides of Lake Zurich and the Wallensee, with the mountains on the sides of the lakes becoming higher and steeper as we headed further east.

The rain had paused briefly by the time we got off the train in Sargans. We found a nearby grocery store and did our first food shopping – crackers, peanut butter and jelly, instant mashed potatoes and noodles, powdered milk, tuna in a foil pouch – whatever we could find that looked light, nutritious, easy to prepare, and reasonably indestructible.

Our last task before we headed for the mountains, and it was a critical one, was to find propane canisters that would fit our tiny MSR "Pocket Rocket" camping stoves. When I bought the stoves in Colorado, I asked the salesman at least four times if the canisters would be available in Europe. He assured me that they would be, since they used a worldwide standard fitting that dozens of the major manufacturers of camp stoves had adopted. Confidently, we started in the camping section of a small department store in Sargans. They sold MSR stoves, but the only propane canisters they carried had the completely different fitting for the Campinggaz brand stoves. The clerk in the department store directed us to a nearby sports store. Again, Campinggaz, but nothing for MSR. The clerk at the sports store was doubtful, but perhaps the appliance store in the neighboring town of Mels would be able to help us. At the appliance store they had more Campinggaz canisters – these were huge, honking 50 pounders – but not what we needed. The clerk was anxious to help us. Perhaps if we went to Migros in Zurich. ...

By this time it was 6 pm, and we had exhausted the likely stores in both towns. We were anxious to get a start on the trail and find someplace to camp before dark. Besides, we were mountain men (and woman) and we would just build campfires for the first few days.

Immediately outside the Sargans train station there had been an information sign for the Via Alpina and footpath signs pointing out the trail. For several miles as we walked through Sargans and Mels, the trail signs were clear. Each time we came to an intersection where a turn was required, there would be another marker. On the outskirts of Mels, however, just as the road started to rise, we reached a T-junction with no sign. The road in each direction ascended steeply, and struggling under the unaccustomed weight of our backpacks we had no desire to walk uphill for several miles to get to a dead-end at a mountain hamlet. Nor did we want to walk 8 miles on the clearly signposted road to Weisstannen, which was the last village we would go through before we hit the big-time high-country. We were anxious to get off the road and onto a genuine Swiss mountain footpath. Unfortunately, our 30-year-old topographical map was of no help at this point.

We walked briefly up the road in one direction, but found no further trail indications. At this point the drizzle, which for the past hour had been dampening our clothes but not yet our spirits, increased to the point where we had to call it rain, and we stopped to put on our rain gear. Within seconds, the rain tapered off; we tried walking for a while with the gear on, but quickly became too hot, so we stopped again and took the gear off. We walked back to the T-junction, and heading off in the other direction we came to a small group of houses. I heard sounds of occupancy from one of the houses, so I knocked on the door. A woman answered and I asked her if she could direct us to the footpath to Weisstannen.

"I just moved here from Romania," she responded in broken German, "I don't know the area." (For hundreds of years Switzerland was notoriously xenophobic, struggling valiantly to keep out foreigners – except, of course, for tourists. Now, however, it seems to be losing that battle, with more than 20% of its 7.5 million population being foreign nationals.)

At a neighboring house, we came upon a woman loading a baby carriage into the trunk of a car. "The road to Weisstannen is that way," she said pointing back in the first direction we had tried.

"But we're looking for the footpath," I responded. She shrugged her shoulders.

We walked on past the houses for another few hundred yards to where the road stopped and a path continued steeply uphill. There we encountered four rustic-types gathered around a panicked, bleating sheep. They greeted us enthusiastically; as we were to discover, Swiss farmers usually seem pleased to see the hikers and campers that are such an important part of their economy.

"Is this the footpath to Weisstannen?" I asked them.

Yes it was, they responded. One of them looked at the setting sun and at the rain clouds and said doubtfully, "But you're not planning on walking there tonight, are you?"

"No," I assured him, "We're going to camp somewhere up on the mountain."

They wished us a good trip and we continued on up the hill, leaving them to whatever unnatural acts they were contemplating with the sheep.

We followed the path into the forest, where it joined a much larger, well-marked trail. The valley narrowed, and as we hiked steadily uphill we were treated to impressive views of the valley floor with a rushing stream far below. On the far slope of the valley we could see the headlights of cars heading up and down the main Weisstannen road.

Even when it's overcast, it stays light fairly late in a Swiss mountain valley on the 19th of June. But clearly it was time for us to find a place to pitch our tents.

Finding a flat spot was not an easy proposition. The trail was consistently rocky and steep, through dense forest. To the right, the ground sloped sharply uphill; to the left it was sharply, often precipitously, downhill. However, after about 90 minutes of careful searching as we walked, I found a small flat clearing just below the trail. It wasn't raining at the moment, but the ground and all the vegetation were thoroughly sodden after days of torrential rains, so we decided to forego trying to build a fire and ate a quick dinner of trail mix and peanut butter and jelly on crackers.

Our First Hill

Starting Our Trip the Hard Way

David   June 22nd-24th

With the late start, we only walked for about 2 hours before Dad found a perfect spot for a campsite and we set up our tents for their first practical use ever.

The tents were the ultra-light, single-wall variety, weighing slightly over a pound each. That's great for carrying on your back, but because they're so thin there's a tremendous build-up of condensation anytime the temperature outside is colder than inside, which is always. Leaving the front flap open helps a little, but in the rain or bitter cold you can't do that, so the inside of the tent drips all night. While it's designed for the drops to run off to the sides and the bottom, Angela's and my tent was not big enough for two people (it would've been perfect for one-and-a-half people), which meant every 3 or 4 minutes we'd brush up against the wall and get hit by an ice-cold patch of water. Since 90% of our bodies were inside our sleeping bags, it was the sleeping bags that usually got hit. They were down-filled, and wet down is a catastrophe to be avoided at all costs; it doesn't keep you warm and takes forever to dry. It was weeks before our paranoia subsided, when we finally realized it would take substantially more water build-up to cause a problem.

Of course, here I'm expounding with the knowledge of 2-months' worth of trekking. At the time we had no earthly clue what we were doing, and I was just happy that I remembered how to set the darn tent up.

It poured like a son of a bitch that first night (in retrospect it was just normal rain; it just seemed like it was pouring because we didn't know any better yet), and by the time we woke up the walls of the tent had sunken in on all sides, all but forming an extra layer of skin around us. Clearly we'd have to figure out how to prevent that in the future. As we drifted awake, Angela and I lay immobile, wondering how the hell we'd get out without touching the sides of the tent. We contemplated staying in bed forever, but decided against that plan since Dad had all the food. So after an hour of negotiating, strategizing, maneuvering, and bending in ways I didn't know was possible, I managed to clamber over Angela and out of the tent, only getting water on three-quarters of our persons and belongings.

By the time we made it out and ate our breakfast of granola and milk, the rain had stopped, and we spent the entire day in the sun.

After a tough uphill start, most of the day was fairly easy walking – mostly up but with some short downhills and a variety of road and trail surfaces through forest and meadows. A layer of clouds formed a blanket over the mountain peaks, but we were low enough that we could look out over a million shades of green all around us and into the valley below as we trekked through the woods and mountainside trails. In the late morning we reached the hamlet of Müli, which wasn't on the map but had a tiny grocery store that presumably served the dozen or so houses we had passed on the road in. Expecting to do our real grocery shopping in Weistannen 45 minutes later (no need to carry the weight any longer than necessary) we bought a few peaches for a late-morning snack and devoured them as we strolled on, the juice dripping off our elbows.

We got to Weistannen right on schedule, and after wandering around for 15 minutes looking for the grocery store, Dad asked a bus driver where it was.

"There's no grocery store in Weistannen," was the reply.

Incredulously, we asked him what people in Weistannen do for groceries. He told us they drive 10 minutes to Müli. Hmm.

Weistannen did have two hotels and a restaurant, so we walked back to the restaurant, ate a large meal there and then headed out, knowing we'd need to make damn sure we got to Elm before we ran out of food at the end of the next day. To complicate matters, our dried food required boiling water, and we still didn't have any propane for our stove.

We thought, ever so briefly, that our problems were solved when we came to a *Schweizer Familie Feuerstelle*, or Swiss Family Fireplace, which had a level field perfect for camping, a rock fireplace with a grill and a little shed with dry wood. It also happened to be right next to a creek, which would give us a chance to do laundry and refill our water bottles. That evening would be our first opportunity to use one of our camping toys, an ultraviolet water purifier called the Steri-Pen. Winner of *Time Magazine*'s "Invention of the Year" award in 2001, it's about the size and weight of a banana and will sterilize a liter of water in 90 seconds. That sure beats carrying gallons on your back day after day.

Leaving Dad to start the fire, Angela and I went to the creek to wash our clothes. When we came back 45 minutes later, we half-expected Dad to have prepared dinner, eaten it and gone to bed, leaving our food in pots on one of the benches. But he had spent the whole time struggling to light the kindling, which after a month of torrential rain was just too wet to catch.

We tried to come to Dad's rescue and managed to blow through an entire lighter full of butane, a tea candle, and half a box of storm-proof matches, all to no avail. We considered giving up and just hydrating the food with cold water and crunch-crunch-crunching away at it, but I wasn't quite that desperate yet.

Dad gave up and started on peanut butter and jelly crackers, but I thought back to starting fires with nothing but dry wood and some wadded up newspaper, so Angela and I decided to give it one last shot. We carefully used the wood to build a platform, and stuffed the two pieces of newspaper from the shed underneath, struggling to light it at first, but ultimately managing to strike up a little wisp of a flame.

"More paper!" Angela threw in our train tickets and started tearing off sheets from the train schedule she'd picked up in Zurich. "More!" We kept adding paper and began to notice that the pine had started to catch. We piled some more wood on top, and added more paper underneath.

Stopping for a moment, we looked at our fledgling fire to determine our next course of action. Dad called over, "Did you get it going?"

"We think so!"

We looked down briefly and discussed whether or not to add more paper. "That's all the paper we've got."

"Yes, but there's not enough for another fire tomorrow, and if we don't get this one going, we've lost our chance."

She tore another page from the train schedule, crumpled it, and threw it in there. The fire grew briefly and then started to stagnate. As we discussed our options, Dad came over and looked at it. "It's trying real hard," I said. "We're wondering if we should move it under the grill."

Dad concurred. "Move it to the center and start blowing on it. You'll have a blazing fire in no time."

And no time later, we had a blazing fire going. We spent the rest of the night marveling over our accomplishment. We decided to make hot chocolate just because, damn it, we could. And we sat by the dying embers as the dusk fell and turned to dark, warming our feet and writing about the beautiful day and the glorious night.

The Day of *The Bad News*

For a while today, I wasn't sure Angela was going to make it.

Dawn broke beautifully with the sun shining. That was a good thing, since the clothes we had washed by the stream were still wet. We hung them over a fence where the sun would get to them. By 9 am they were still not completely dry, but we needed to get on the trail. So we changed into the still damp clothes, figuring they would dry on our bodies as we walked, and headed up the hill.

After a few minutes' walk, we hit the big-time uphill and for the next 3 hours we walked steadily up. At first we were on the side of the mountain, high above the valley floor and its cascading stream, but later the valley floor came up to meet us.

Angela walks uphill very slowly, and try as hard as I might, I just couldn't seem to go at that pace. So every 20 minutes or so I would look up and realize that I was alone. I would find a place to sit down and wait for her and David to catch up. Sometimes it would take as much as 20 minutes for them to appear. Then David would scold me for not staying with them and we'd start off again, together at first, but in a few minutes I would have left them behind and the process would start all over.

Just before noon, we came to a place where the trail was blocked by a rushing stream, perhaps 20 feet wide. I could see the path continuing on the other side, but there seemed to be no easy way to get across without going into the stream knee deep or worse. I'd had enough experience with wet boots during my trek across Britain to know that it was not something I wanted to risk, and I started surveying up and down the bank for a better spot to cross. David, on the other hand, is a bouncy animal (picture Tigger from *Winnie the*

Pooh) and is all for just forging ahead in situations like this. By the time I had found my spot, David was already sitting on the other side of the bank sunbathing with a bored look on his face. Eventually I made my way across, and as David crossed back over to help Angela, I climbed up a small rise to make sure we were on the right trail. I immediately realized that we weren't. Apparently the main trail had turned off several hundred yards earlier. But I often tend not to notice things like that, either being hypnotized by the scenery and the rhythm of walking, or concentrating on singing snatches of relevant songs like "I Love to Go A-wandering Along the Mountain Track" or "They Call the Wind Mariah" at the top of my lungs. While David castigated me mercilessly for not walking with them – overall we had spent about a half-hour on our little detour – he crossed the stream a third time to pick up his pack, and then we both made our way back across the stream and down to the trail fork.

Whereas farther down there had been cows all over the trail, now there were goats. We frequently had to push them out of the way to get past. Note that we are talking about a very steep, narrow, rocky mountain trail, so walking around them was not an option. Just as we got to a particularly steep section where the trail actually turned into a set of steps going virtually straight up, we had to stand aside for four men carrying mountain bikes to come down past us. At this point we were probably 4 miles up from anything I would consider remotely cyclable, and as we went on it was another 4 miles before it got cyclable again. These guys either managed to cycle straight up and straight down an impossibly steep and narrow mountain track, or they carried their bikes for 8 miles over 1,500 feet of rise and drop.

Fifteen minutes later we came to a mountain hut with two dozen people sitting outside drinking and chatting. As we took a break to snack on some trail mix, I chatted with one of the hikers. Then, in the 5 minutes it took us to fill up our water bottles, everyone was gone, having headed off in one direction or the other. Next to the hut were an ambiguous trail sign and a forking path, and it was unclear which was the trail to the Foopass. After a brief discussion, we followed the path that most of the ascending hikers had taken.

All day, we had been walking up a steep, narrow canyon next to the rushing torrent of the stream. At this point though, the canyon widened out to a splendid upland valley, surrounded on three sides by tall, craggy mountains. The only way out appeared to be a saddle between two of the peaks; the saddle was perhaps a half-mile long and broken into two depressions with a smaller peak between them. The trail we were on was heading for the right-hand depression. After another 90 minutes of climbing, we came to a tiny mountain hut with several people sunning themselves in front of it. To verify that we were on the right path, I asked a young lady, "Geht dieser Weg nach dem Foopass?" ("Is this the path for the Foopass?")

"Oh, nein, für Foopass muessen Sie dort drüben gehen." ("Oh no, for Foopass you have to go over there.") And she pointed across the deep valley to another ridge that led to the left-hand depression in the wall sealing the head of the valley.

We're supposed to be over *there*?

At this point Angela, who was clearly tired from 3 days of backpacking, including nearly 3,000 feet of vertical climbing over more than 4 hours that day, almost lost it. I realized that if, instead of climbing down into the valley and up the other side, we continued toward the right-hand side of the saddle we could eventually make our way around the edge of the cliff wall to where the trail exited over the top of the pass. Nonetheless, as we started bushwhacking up the slope, Angela was having only moderate success in concealing a steady flow of tears behind her sunglasses. But after she off-loaded some weight, with David taking her sleeping bag and me taking her ground pad, her spirits improved. For the next hour we worked our way across open slope past snowfields, over streams and through upland marshes. By 2:15 we trudged up the last few hundred yards and plopped down next to the signpost marking the knife-edge top of the Foopass. The view in the direction we were heading was truly awesome – craggy snow covered peaks, steep-sided canyons, lush green valleys, and everywhere cascading waterfalls.

We ate the last of our food – peanut butter and jelly and crackers, tuna fish in a foil pouch, a dried sausage, and some chocolate. By the time we struggled into our packs again it was 3:15. The walk to Elm was supposed to have been 6 hours. Instead, after 6 hours we were just starting what promised to be a long, hard descent. Over the next 3 hours, we dropped 4,000 feet and walked (hobbled?) into the town of Elm.

We had been on the trail for 3 days, and after 9 hours of walking that day we were in dire need of a cooked meal, hot showers and beds. We were lucky enough to find rooms in a small hotel. My room was very basic, only big enough for the bed, a chair and a sink. The shower and toilet were elsewhere – the shower upstairs and down the hall, and the toilet off a landing a floor and a half down. Not that that was a problem; with a room of that size you can pee in the sink without getting out of bed.

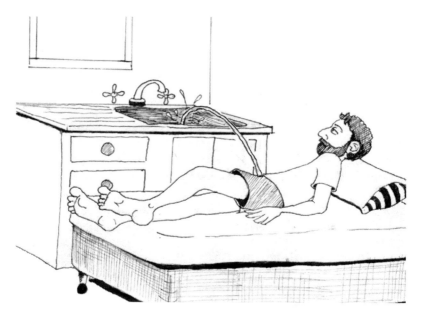

But what it lacked in accommodation, it made up for in price. David and Angela's room, only marginally bigger than mine, was nearly $100. That being said, nearly everything in Switzerland is extortionately expensive. Everything, that is, except for pitching a tent beside a stream and eating granola and powdered milk and peanut butter and jelly on crackers.

We had an excellent but overpriced dinner. I was mightily impressed that Angela had managed to survive (and to not kill me for leading them on the long detour on the path up to the Foopass), and made it a point to tell her so while we were waiting for our food. Meanwhile, David was nearly catatonic from the shock to his system of the past 3 days. When the food came, he sat for a minute with a dazed expression on his face and then he started toying with his meal, putting an occasional fork of meat or potatoes into his mouth and chewing slowly. Recognizing a potential opportunity, I wolfed down my macaroni, hoping that he would not finish his food and I would get to eat what was left over. No such luck. Eventually he got going and cleaned his plate. Even he had to admit, though, that he had not displayed his usual culinary enthusiasm. He vowed to do better in the days to come.

After dinner we went upstairs to take showers and make use of hot running water to wash our sweaty clothes. Then I went downstairs to use a phone to call my wife, Rhonda, at her apartment in Austin, and my mother in California. By 10 pm I was lying in bed using my headlamp (there was only one dim light bulb in the room, and it was over the sink) to write my nightly letter. Nearly every night throughout the trek I wrote long, newsy letters on what we were experiencing. Most of the time that involved lying on my back in my sleeping bag in the tent, trying to convince my ballpoint pen to continue writing upside down. Periodically, I'd mail the letters back to my house in Colorado, where my house-sitters, Molly and Walker, would scan them into the computer and e-mail them to a list of 20 or so friends and family around the world.

The Day of *The Bad News* – Redux

David   June 24th

Angela just about killed Dad when she found out that we were on the wrong side of the valley. Of course she knew that it wasn't in any way his fault, but we were already pissed at him for walking ahead of us, so she had no problem making him a scapegoat for the time being as we trudged on, our legs getting heavier with every step.

For the previous couple of hours I'd been offering her no shortage of encouragement: "We're almost there. We've gone up 2,000 feet, only a few hundred more left." Indeed, whenever we looked back at where we'd come from, the views and our sense of accomplishment were nothing short of stunning. And periodically, when I was particularly convinced that she was struggling, I would ask her, "Heaven or Hell?" to which she would look around, realize what an extraordinary experience this was, and respond, "Heaven," with a glowing look of satisfaction.[3]

After receiving *The Bad News*, however, my words of encouragement were more often met with a hysterical "WHAT DO YOU MEAN IT'S NOT THAT BAD!!! I CAN'T EVEN FEEL MY

---

[3] Heathrow airport has a series of ads for HSBC (Hong Kong Shanghai Bank Corporation) that highlight the differences in people's points of view: for example, a photo of a chili pepper with the word PLEASURE imposed over it; next to it a photo of a high-heeled shoe, with the word PAIN. Next to that, the chili pepper with the word PAIN, and next to that the high-heeled shoe with the word PLEASURE. There were dozens of these all over the airport. Particularly poignant were Work/Play (a laptop and a baby) and Holiday/Hell (a guy in a tent and people on a cruise) which more or less epitomize the differences between Mom and Dad. Guess which one Dad thinks is a holiday. Anyway, the Heaven/Hell contrast became the theme of the trip.

LEGS AND WE HAVE TO CLIMB ANOTHER TEN THOUSAND FEET!!" Needless to say, my "Heaven or Hell?" question was not met with quite so enthusiastic a response as it had been earlier in the day.

Our agony was given a hiatus during our long overdue lunch, but it was only about 15 minutes into our 3 hour descent that my toes started hurting, and after an hour my feet were in so much pain that I had to consciously hide the grimace on my face whenever Angela or Dad turned to look at me. By the halfway point, I had to consciously make the effort to stop checking my watch every 3 minutes.

Sitting in the restaurant, exhausted and sun burnt, I pounded back the first beer they put in front of me, and ravenously ordered a second. Removing my hiking boots, I dug around for about 3 or 4 minutes in my backpack, with the other restaurant patrons looking on in curiosity to see what it was this pathetic, barely conscious soul so desperately sought at the bottom of his pack. The entire restaurant shared a good laugh when I pulled out my Crocs.

I have in my notes that I showered, washed my clothes, hung them in the window, and then sat in bed writing. Quite honestly, I don't remember any of that, and exhausted as I was, I'm amazed I was able to do anything but just collapse in the hope that tomorrow's rest day would be enough for us to recover from this brutal start to our trip.

More Adventures With Fire

David   **June 25th-26th**

"Just when the caterpillar thought the world was going to end, it turned into a butterfly." *Anonymous*

In retrospect, starting our trip with a 12-hour, 19-mile hike with 5,700 feet of vertical gain might not have been the most prudent of decisions. Having barely survived it, we were all looking forward to a well-deserved rest day – particularly Angela, who was not exactly raring to go and climb another 4,000 feet any time soon.

Things got more complicated when everyone we talked to informed us that a snowstorm was on its way, and that if we didn't go over the Richetlipass that day we'd have to wait another 2 or 3 days to leave. For a moment, we thought the world was going to end, hyperventilating at the thought of walking another 8 feet, much less 80,000.

Fortunately, we were able to find the one computer in Elm with Internet access – an ancient PC in a hotel. The PC room was usually closed on Mondays, but the proprietor made a special exception and opened it up just for us. We looked at the Via Alpina website and a couple of maps and found a much more desirable plan. We'd spend the night at a municipal campsite we'd passed on our way into town; then in the morning we'd take a bus halfway around the mountain to Schwanden, walk the rest of the way (on a flat trail) to Linthal, and take a cable car up to Braunwald where we could have a day or two of moderate walking before our next big climb.

We loaded up on groceries and hiked the 15 minutes back up to the campsite. On the way, I asked Dad about the local greeting, *grüezi,* that he'd been exchanging with people for the last several days. (For those of you who are unfamiliar with Swiss German, about the best I can do for you is to tell you that it's pronounced as though you're saying "GROOT-see" while vomiting.) When saying hello to multiple people, it's "Grüezi mit ein ander," which means "Greetings with one another." I wasn't yet familiar with the phrase, and asked Dad what it was he was saying. He spelled it out with the rhythm of the Mickey Mouse song. "M-I-T ... E-I-N ... A-N-D-E-R ... Mit ein ander, Donald Duck!" (It was really funny, I swear. I guess you had to be there.)

We got to the campsite around 12:30 and, since it was in the woods, spent some time searching for a root-free spot. Dad found one in a clearing, and Angela and I found one that was free of roots but overrun by slugs, so instead we opted for a partially rootified spot where we set up camp and then went to work on lunch.

This time, we didn't have any problem finding tinder that would light. Rather, our difficulty was that it started to drizzle almost immediately. Angela suggested covering the fire, which we thought was a ridiculously stupid idea, but that didn't stop us from trying. Dad pulled out a thin plastic poncho that he's been carrying around in his hiking emergency kit for 7 years and never used (he thought it was a ground cloth until we opened it up), and we took turns, two of us holding it over the fireplace, taking gasps of air between clouds of smoke as the third knelt below building the fire.

As the fire started to grow, Angela backed off and Dad and I stood there, holding the poncho over the fire.

"Now what?"

Angela suggested propping up the poncho with sticks. Once again, we thought she was out of her tiny little mind, but I didn't live to the ripe age of 26 by questioning my fiancée's ideas.

She grabbed a long stick, managed to prop it up between a rock and the fireplace, and hooked the hood over the end of it. Now we only needed one person to hold the poncho up. We continued to find rocks and sticks, using the one to prop up the other and rubber bands to tie the edges of the poncho around the edges of the sticks.

By 2:00 we had a raging fire, completely protected from the rain that would continue through the afternoon and evening. We admitted to Angela that yes, she was the goddess of fire, and we were but humble apprentices in comparison. (Dad started to develop a serious inferiority complex, since he'd had years of experience building fires as a Boy Scout, but thus far had been completely shown up on the fire-building front. The next morning while Angela and I were writing he built a fire by himself, just to prove to himself he could.)

The Gang In Front of Our Sheltered Fire

We cooked lunch, and then almost immediately after we were done eating, began on dinner. For dessert we had Ovomaltine, a local brand of chocolate malted drink that tastes mostly like chocolate piss. We had bought a box with 10 servings and made three of them that night, two a couple of nights later, and then just carried the rest around with us day after day, convinced that we would drink them eventually but never quite being able to stomach the thought of ingesting any more of that nauseating concoction.

Three weeks later we convinced ourselves to throw them away.

Seeing the storm moving its way through the valley, over the town, and heading straight toward us, we got into our tents and hunkered down for the night. As the rain poured down, it took Angela and me about 2 hours to waterproof our tent, climbing out to readjust the tent poles and stakes, and setting our rain pants and jackets under the edges of the ground cloth so the rain would go underneath the ground cloth instead of on top of it.

The rain hitting the outside of our tent splashed condensation from the inside onto our faces, but we just had to put up with it and go to sleep. The thunder rolled over us through the night. The rain soaked through to our souls. We woke up aching, tired and sore from an uncomfortable night of sleep, but also relieved and somewhat encouraged by having survived the storm.

As Angela and I sat on a bench overlooking the town to write, we stared out at the clouds, which had settled in on the valley. Through the occasional break, we could spot the mountain peaks off in the distance, where the precipitation had fallen as snow, but mostly the clouds obscured the entire mountain before us. A little black kitten bounded through the meadow before us; perhaps it was as delighted as we were to have made it through the night. Dad rebuilt the fire underneath the poncho shelter, which had miraculously withstood the storm. Time for another day.

There were two sports stores in Elm. The previous morning we had visited both, and neither had the propane that would fit our campstove. Both suggested that we try the sports stores in Schwanden for the gas canister we needed. So after breakfast we broke camp and took the bus to Schwanden, where we were told there weren't any sports stores – perhaps we should try in Elm. Hmm.

We spent the rest of the morning and the early afternoon hiking to Linthal, following signs for the *Fridliweg*. Weg is German for "way" (as in "path" or "trail"), and as near we could tell from the pictures of a monk wearing a robe and carrying a book and a staff, the Fridliweg followed some kind of pilgrimage route. Regardless, the monk, whom we dubbed Fridli, was unassailably cute, which led to Angela calling me her little Friedli. I'll pause for a moment while you go off into the other room and barf. We later found out that Fridli was the mascot for Glarus, the canton[4] we were walking through at the time.

Glarus Fridli

When we got to Linthal, Dad asked someone where we might get the gas we need. She suggested we might be able to find something in a store 2 miles further up the road in the wrong direction. Thank you, no. As luck would have it, though, we actually found the right canister an hour later in Braunwald, a car-free "spa resort" 700 yards up the aptly-named Braunwaldbahn funicular[5]. The propane tank was about three times the size we wanted – but it fit the campstove, so we took it cheerfully and headed on up the path toward our next stage destination.

Along the way we found another *Schweizer Familie Feuerstelle* (Swiss Family Fireplace), always great for making fires, but in this

---

[4] Switzerland is divided into 26 cantons, which were historically sovereign states that united over a period of about 7 centuries. More on that later.

[5] A funicular is a train that goes up a steep incline on the ground, aided either by cables or by cog gears underneath the train. That is in contrast to a cable car or a gondola, which is suspended on cables high above the ground.

case not so great in terms of campsites. There was a fireplace in the middle of a tiny clearing surrounded by trees, with roots climbing every which way and making for no even spots in the whole area. After a few minutes of exploring, we discovered our options were to try to build bunk beds out of the benches next to the fireplace or to pitch our tent across the way, in a field that was ankle deep in cow shit.

Angela and I spent well over an hour trying to pitch our tent so that one of us could sleep on the bench and the other on the ground next to it. We tried everything we could to get the tent both high enough and wide enough to keep the edges from touching the person on the top bunk. Dad, meanwhile, who had long since set up his own tent in the cow field, had explored the area enough to show us another spot only moderately fecularized, which he felt would work better than our bunk.

Being partially swayed by Dad's suggestion, Angela and I stood in the field near tears, and changed our minds three times before Dad finally reappeared from the Feuerstelle with our tent, and we resigned ourselves to our fate. Following Dad's example, we used our plastic shit-shovel (normally used for digging holes to bury our own feculences) to clear the plot, and spent the night nestled nicely in our bed of mud and scooped out cow dung as the rain pissed down on us for a second straight night.

Even though it wasn't particularly bad – by which I mean there was no smell – we were convinced that the cows would eventually make their way back and try eating our tents in the middle of the night. After about half an hour, though, we decided to make the best of the situation by snuggling in close for the rest of the night. Still, Angela swore she would never forgive us for making her sleep in Farmer Fritz's Patty Patch.

Bovine Tinnitus

Don   **June 27**[th]

I had retreated to my tent the night before at 9 pm. Even under the best of circumstances there's not a lot to do after the sun goes down when you are camping. But these were not the best of circumstances. The rain, which had been intermittent all afternoon, became steady and increased in intensity, and the temperature dropped quickly to near freezing and stayed there all night.

In spite of spending 8½ hours in my sleeping bag, I probably got no more than 5 hours of sleep. While the spot where I had pitched my tent was the best available under the circumstances, it had more of a slope and more rocks and bumps than I would have liked. Since the tent floor, the sleeping pad and the sleeping bag were all extremely smooth, any slope resulted in my sliding downhill. That night, with a significant slope, was a serious struggle. The only things that kept me from sliding out of the tent and 2,000 feet down to valley floor were the facts that: a) I had pitched the tent just above a large boulder; and b) David's full backpack was at my feet. (Because Angela and David's tent was extremely crowded, they stored some of their excess gear in mine, especially in wet weather.) Each time I managed to doze off for a few minutes, the backpack would slide down the hill until it came to rest against the boulder, and I would slide down until I was crumpled in a heap against the backpack. Then I'd drag myself back up to a more or less standing position with my feet braced against the pack and try to get back to sleep.

Since the sleeping pad, which is a thin foam pad with an inflatable air-tight casing around it, is only about an inch thick, the rocks and dirt mounds were another challenge. Considering the obstacles, I was surprised that I got as much sleep as I did. It's wonderful what walking 6 to 8 hours a day in the mountains with a pack on your back and granola and instant mashed potatoes in your belly will do for you.

At 5:30 am I awoke to the two best pieces of news I'd had in days. First, everything inside the tent had stayed reasonably dry. And second, for the moment at least, it was not raining. I emerged from my tent to see the edge of the sun breaking through the clouds as it rose over the crest of a snow-covered peak at the end of the valley far to the east. The sky overhead wasn't clear yet, but the cloud cover overhead was definitely showing signs of breaking.

There were no sounds of life from Angela and David's tent. I wasn't sure if they were still asleep, engaging in particularly silent extra-curricular activities, or were frozen solid encased in ice. I knew better than to interfere if they were asleep or engaging in extra-curriculars. And if they were frozen, there wasn't much I could do about it, other than perhaps pilfering Angela's micro-fiber towels which I'd been coveting since we started the walk.

I made my way down the hill to sit on one of the Feuerstelle benches to wait for them and to contemplate what I'd learned in the first week of our trek:

First, on Swiss footpath navigation. At nearly every road or trail intersection there are yellow footpath direction signs. They usually give the name of the destinations for that route, the level of difficulty (a red and white stripe indicates a *Bergweg*, or mountain path) and sometimes give the walking time. Occasionally we'd find signs for a Panoramaweg or a Fridliweg or some other kind of weg. Of course, as on nearly all trails, sometimes we would get to a fork with no sign, particularly in the mountains where there are generally fewer markings than in the lower country. Then we would take a guess, which was wrong as often as it was right. To supplement Tomas's 40-year-old topographical maps, we were stopping in at tourist offices to pick up brochures, which often had small scale pictorial trail maps. If we got really lost, I had a small GPS, the size of an old-fashioned pocket watch, which we'd used once several days ago, but wouldn't need again for the rest of the trip. For the first couple of days we had seen Via Alpina signs on the signposts along with all the other way markers. The previous day, however, they had disappeared. We hoped they would reappear soon.

Second, on cowbells. Cows in Switzerland all carry huge, heavy bells around their necks. The bells make a terrific clanging every time the cows move, and the sound can be heard for miles. If you've got a herd of cattle, the clamor is deafening. Trying to sleep nearby, as we were last night, can be maddening. I was having visions of myself hunched over with a big lump on my back, a mouth full of bad teeth and my hands clasped over my ears screaming "The bells, the bells."

A lot of cows complain about that ringing in their ears.
Perhaps the Bovine Tinnitus Society can help.

And third, on the routine of finding campsites and making and breaking camp. A great deal of time and mental effort was spent trying to find a suitable place. Is this spot flat enough? Is there water nearby? Is camping allowed here, or will the farmer come and kick us out after dark in the rain? If it starts to rain, will we be in the path of a stream or on a flood plain? When we finally decided on a campsite, off came the pack and out came the tent. It could be set up in about 3 minutes – 1 pole and 4 stakes. Then I'd unroll my inflatable sleeping pad and blow it up, take my sleeping bag out of its stuff sack so the down would have time to fluff out before bed and unpack the rest of my gear and lay it out on the floor of the tent. Total elapsed time, about 8 minutes.

Breaking camp in the morning was a much longer and more complicated operation. For one thing, the inside and outside of the tent were both generally dripping wet from rain and/or condensation. So I'd get out my micro-fiber towel and start wiping the tent walls and wringing out the towel and repeating the process until the tent was dry enough to roll. Then I'd flip it over and dry the underside of the floor and roll it tightly enough that, after a struggle, it would fit into its sack. In the meantime, I'd deflate the sleeping pad, roll it, put it in its stuff sack, and tie a cord around the outside to keep it small. The sleeping bag had its own high-tech stuff sack that squeezed the bag into a sphere about 8 inches in diameter. Then all the rest of the gear and clothing had to go into waterproof bags and the bags had to go in the backpack in exactly the right positions and order. Otherwise, the backpack would end up full but there'd still be gear strewn on the ground. The tent and sleeping pad got strapped to the outside of the backpack and the two water bottles were filled and put into the side pockets. Elapsed time, 60-75 minutes, depending on how wet the tent had been. And that didn't include preparing and eating breakfast and cleaning up afterward. Or doing our personal ablutions. Often, I'd wake up at 6:30 and it would be 9:00-9:30 before we were ready to hit the trail. Life can be hard when you're a mountain man.

By 7:30 the weather was closing in again, so I decided to take a chance on waking up – or thawing out – Angela and David. It didn't look as though they had been asleep or frozen, which left only one alternative. Under those conditions? Wow!

I'm sure the walk down to the village of Urnerboden would have been beautiful if we could have seen anything. As it was, the fog was so dense that all we could see was the narrow trail leading up and down the side of an extremely steep slope. The trail in many places had been trampled by cattle, and with all the rain we'd had in the past several days, it was a muddy mess. Because of the steepness of the terrain, we had to stick to the trail, which meant wading through ankle deep mud for several miles.

Urnerboden looked as though it was once far more prosperous than it is now. There was a cable car up the side of a nearby mountain with a sign saying that it ran only on demand, but we couldn't find anybody to demand it from. The post office and tourist information center had closed down, and the bus over the Klausenpass wouldn't start running until July. Other than a few houses, the center of the village had little more than a hotel, a couple of small restaurants, and of course, the omnipresent church.

In a wing of the church was a tiny grocery store, where we stopped to re-supply. Buying groceries is a lot simpler when the store is all of 200 square feet. The clerk commiserated with us about the prospect of continuing our trek in the pouring rain and suggested that we ask at the farmhouses along the road up toward the Klausenpass if we could sleep in their barns. As we climbed the road from Urnerboden toward the pass, the rain came pouring down harder than anything we had yet encountered. Being well used to rain from 20 years of hiking in England, I put my head down and plodded on as stoically as I could. Meanwhile, Angela looked more miserable with every step. David says he was just as miserable, but as he's a bouncy animal, it's often hard to tell with him.

After about 45 minutes we came upon a tiny farmer's hut with a barn next to it. An elderly lady in an apron saw me approaching and came to the door to greet me. She had a stocky, powerful build, and her face and hands had the timeless, weathered look of someone who has spent 60 years working in the rain and the wind. I explained our plight to her while David and Angela waited in the front yard looking pathetic, and she agreed let us sleep in the straw in the loft of her barn. While we were waiting for her husband to come in from tending the cows, she invited us into the stone floor entrance-hall/mud room which also functioned as the kitchen. We took off our wet rain gear and shoes and went into the one room bedroom/living room/dining room to sit and warm ourselves by leaning against a wall which backed onto the huge cast-iron cooking stove.

After an hour, her 76-year-old husband arrived. He was as lean and sinewy as she was stocky, but with the same weather-beaten skin. With him was a handsome young man, whom I assumed was their son. He was tall and slender, with long, dark hair, and large, dramatic eyes; come to think of it, he looked a lot like a young Jeff Goldblum. I'm afraid I'll have to continue referring to them as the couple and the young man; although I introduced myself several times, they declined to give their names. It turned out that the young man was an Italian movie projectionist from South Tyrol[6] who had decided to work for a summer as a farm laborer in Switzerland. He confided to us in English, which the couple could not understand, that he was very unhappy with his situation. All he did was work 16 hours a day and eat and sleep the other eight. He had been there since the first of June and was scheduled to stay on until the beginning of September; he was already counting the days until he could leave.

We learned from him that the hut is the couple's spring and fall quarters. As soon as the weather was warm enough, which would be in about another week, they would move with the cattle several thousand feet higher up the pass to another hut. The couple have 20 cows, which produce 75 gallons of milk a day. Each day, a truck comes by to pick up the milk and take it to the nearest dairy cooperative. In the late autumn, they walk with the cattle 20 miles over the Klausenpass to their winter quarters in Spiringen, near Altdorf. The couple also tend several pigs. I don't know if pigs can make a trek like that on foot (pig feet?). Presumably if they have not ended up as part of a schnitzel by then, they are taken over the pass by truck.

We waited while the couple and the young man had their afternoon meal. The Italian apologized profusely for the couple's

---

[6] South Tyrol is a German-speaking province in northern Italy. Just across the border to the north is the Austrian province of Tyrol.

rudeness in not offering us food, and I admit I was a bit surprised at first. Considering the Spartan nature of the cabin and the couple's existence there though, it would have been surprising if they had offered us anything. In any case, we would have politely declined any offer.

After their meal, our host showed us to our quarters in the loft of the barn. To access the loft, we could either climb a precarious wooden ladder to the main doors in the front of the barn, or go in the back door and climb up a nearly-as-precarious ladder. We were so delighted to be out of the rain and lying on soft, clean straw, that we immediately flopped down and took a nap. It was certainly tough 2 hours later to convince ourselves to get up and go into the kitchen/entrance hall, which our hostess had offered us the use of, to heat up and eat our dinner of canned ravioli and string beans.

By 7 pm we were back up in our loft and ready for bed. Because it was still raining and cold and windy, I closed the front doors, which locked from the outside, and came in the back way. Some time later, when our host came in the back way to get some supplies for the animals, he wished us a good night's rest. Around midnight I got up to use the crude outhouse next to the barn and went down the back way to find that we had been locked in. I stood there in an uncomfortable panic, trying to decide whether to pee in one of the feed buckets, before I remembered that the lock was a simple hook on the outside of the door. After trying several tools that were lying around, I found a scythe that would fit through the doorframe and managed to lift the hook and escape to the outhouse. What a relief!

The Exorcism

After spending a week away from civilization, your mind starts to do funny things and often just runs away from you. When we first entered the mud room and our frau encouraged us to leave everything there and come into the kitchen, I became paranoid that they intended to search through all our stuff and steal whatever they thought was useful. Of course, I knew I was just being silly. Then I saw the Italian, staring at us with a strange look on his face. Surely I was just imagining things. But by the time they locked us into the barn, I had become convinced that they were planning on keeping us in there and fattening us up to eat. The whole thing seemed like something out of a Stephen King novel: pouring rain, ghost town with only one open shop, and the lady there suggests we can sleep in the barn of some old farmers ... . I started to feel like we were in the first act of what would soon be the Based On a True Story *Swiss Chainsaw Massacre* or something.

Of course I realized how ridiculous all this was, and never took any of these paranoid delusions seriously. Until, that is, the next morning when we woke up to the sound of an exorcism.

At first I thought it was a dream. After being in the complete darkness of the inside of the barn for 12 hours, I'd started to lose track of the difference between sleeping and being awake. So here I was, in a state of semi-consciousness with this deep, grunting noise combined with a cacophony of high pitched squeals.

As the noise got louder and louder, my eyes started to widen, and by the time I realized I was, in fact awake, the caterwaul had reached a deafening roar. My heart pounded, I started sweating heavily, and I began strategizing how to escape; whether it was better to run or just lie there in silence so the demons didn't notice us. Just as I was getting ready to search through the barn for a wooden stake, the farmer came in and let out the pigs for feeding time. I can't express the sense of relief I felt at that moment, to discover that the sound effects were being made by a group of hungry animals anticipating breakfast and not a possessed family member.

When we were ready to leave, Dad asked our hostess if he could give her any money. She said that she had discussed it with her husband and they'd decided to ask for 3 francs per person (about $2.60). Dad gave her 20 francs and said, "Please take it." She was delighted, and told us that she knew from our faces that we were honest people. As we were leaving, she came out to the edge of her property and pointed out a better route for us to take up to the Klausenpass – a disused gravel farm road, quicker than the paved road and more pleasant than the *Wanderweg* (footpath), which would be ankle deep in mud after 3 weeks of rain.

The previous 2 days of storms had produced a gorgeous layer of snow on the mountain peaks all around us, which we admired during the 90-minute hike up to the top of the pass. Naturally, once we got to the Klausenpass it was time to eat (it's always time to eat), so Angela and I bought a pastry from the snack bar before we started our descent.

Crossing over to the west side of the pass, we realized that we were heading into a very different part of the country. Whereas we'd spent every minute of the previous week in cow pastures, all the farms we passed now were hayfields. Every now and then we'd see a single cow fenced in next to a house, no doubt to provide a single family's milk, butter, cheese, and (after 15 or so years) what I would imagine to be some really tough, crappy-tasting steak and hamburgers. So rather than spending all our time and effort dodging the cow patties, we were able to spend it on more productive activities, like discussing which comic books we liked best, whether *Dave* or *Groundhog Day* was the better movie, and whether the scenery was more reminiscent of Maine or of the "Do-Re-Mi" scene from *The Sound of Music*.

The sun had stayed out most of the day, so when we stopped for lunch we were able to lay out our tents (which had been soaking wet for 4 days) to dry them. By the time we reached Bürglen, home of William Tell and the birthplace of Switzerland, we'd walked 13 miles in 10 hours and were more than ready to crash. Even the sound of two dozen locals drinking and carousing at the top of their lungs outside our hotel window wasn't enough to keep us awake past 10 pm.

Is That an Apple on Your Head?

Don   **June 28th-29th**

After our first week of hiking, we had determined that there was nothing essential we had forgotten to bring. But we had experienced some breakage and lossage (?!) that needed to be remedied before we headed back into the mountains. Over the past week we had encountered only a couple of one-room sports stores, and they invariably did not carry what we needed. Other than those, we had to resign ourselves to searching vainly through the "miscellaneous" shelves of tiny general stores. As we trudged into the prosperous town of Bürglen, we were delighted to come upon a large Inter-Sport store that was a revelation. It had EVERYTHING!

The staff of the store were apparently used to muddy, unkempt backpackers, and showed no signs of surprise or distress when we dragged ourselves in. They were, however, all interested in hearing about our trek – where we had walked from that day, where and when we had started the whole walk, where we would go the next day, where our eventual goal was.

"Where have you come from?"

"Sargans."

"Where are you headed?"

"Mont Blanc."

"!!!!!!!!!"

At this point Mont Blanc was still a month's trek to the west, and playing the Mont Blanc card in our conversations with the locals always got that sort of reaction. A month later, we would substitute saying we were heading to Mont Blanc with saying we had started at the border with Liechtenstein. It worked just as well, even better actually, since by that time instead of being an aspiration it was already a significant achievement.

We spent an hour in the store getting one of my ancient trekking poles repaired, replacing worn out and missing rubber tips (used for road walking) for the poles, buying a new water bottle (the top of one of mine had cracked), and getting a can of waterproofing spray for shoes and jackets and pants that had been severely tested over the previous week.

The manager of the sports store informed us that the nearest public campsite was in Flüelen, on the other side of Altdorf and another 3-mile walk. By this time, we were all exhausted and hungry enough to accept his recommendation of the 600 year-old hotel Zum Adler across the street.

In my semi-official capacity as translator, and in order not to overwhelm the proprietors with filthy, exhausted backpackers, I left David and Angela in front of the hotel and trudged up the stairs to the restaurant. As in most of the other hotels we had been in, the restaurant bar doubled as the hotel reception desk, and the only people in the restaurant were the owners, help, and a couple of local regulars sitting at a table near the cash register smoking and drinking. (The no smoking regulations that the rest of the civilized world has adopted over the past 20 years have apparently not penetrated the Swiss Alps.) All heads turned to stare at me. By now I should have been used to the "What planet did these weirdoes drop in from?" stare whenever we went into a restaurant or hotel, but it still made me uncomfortable.

After showers and laundry, I went downstairs to call Rhonda and my mother back in the States. There was no pay phone, so I asked the owner if I could use the hotel phone to make a toll-free call through my long-distance international phone service.

"No," he responded, "I won't know how much to charge you."

"It will be billed to my credit card."

"But I won't know how much to bill to your credit card."

"You don't have to do it. It goes automatically to my credit card."

"Then how will I get my money?"

"You won't need to get paid. It doesn't cost you anything."

"But you're using my phone."

After fifteen minutes of this he threw up his hands and let me use the phone. I don't think that even then he understood, but I was incredibly persistent and some people think I have an honest face.

By the time I'd finished my calls it was time for dinner. Angela, David and I went down to the restaurant to replace a few thousand calories deficit that we'd built up over the past several days. It's amazing how good food tastes after 10 hours of walking in the mountains carrying a backpack.

The first thing we did the next morning was go to the William Tell Museum, which was in a 12th century tower around the corner from the hotel. According to legend, Tell was a native of Bürglen, and the whole Tell story is supposed to have taken place down the hill in Altdorf and on the lake just to the north of it. The museum featured an excellent narrated slideshow which made strong connections between the lives of the 13th century Swiss and the mountain farmers of today.

In actuality, there may never have been a William Tell who refused to bow to the bailiff's hat, had to shoot an apple off his son's head, was arrested and escaped while being rowed across the lake to prison. What is certain is that in 1291, representatives of three Swiss cantons signed a pact to defend themselves against outside control and to ensure they had a say in their own governance. The other certainty is that the William Tell legend is omnipresent around the world and especially here in Switzerland. Tell has become a recognized symbol of courage and strength, and the slideshow and the museum exhibition displayed hundreds of examples of Tell-labeled products from breakfast cereals to packing crates to financial services.

After the museum, we took the short walk down the hill to Altdorf, a splendid small city that dates back to the end of the first millennium, full of beautifully restored old buildings around cobblestone squares. Since it's at the northern end of the St. Gotthard Pass, one of the main trade routes between northern and southern Europe for the last 700 years, it has been a much sought after piece of real estate.

Altdorf was bustling. Shoppers rushed in and out of the hundreds of small shops, and the sidewalk restaurants and cafes were full of locals basking in the brief sunny respite from a month of rain. In the central square workmen were erecting a marquee for some kind of local festival the next day, while waiters from nearby restaurants sprinted back and forth setting up food stands. After a week of tiny villages and hamlets it was quite a shock.

We went to Migros (the Swiss equivalent of Super Wal-Mart) to fulfill the promise I had made to Rhonda (and to my mother and Rhonda's sisters and Elena and every other female that I had spoken with in the past 2 months) to buy a cell phone that would work in the Alps in case we needed one in an emergency. Since we wouldn't often have access to electrical outlets to charge the phone, I would turn it on only when I needed to make an outgoing call.

After Migros, we wandered around Altdorf a bit, had a leisurely lunch and went to the tourist information office to inquire about local campsites and the route for the next Via Alpina stage over the Surenenpass to Engleberg. Talk about Swiss efficiency! Absolutely every question we asked, the clerk (whom David dubbed "a minx") pulled out a detailed brochure that had exactly what we needed. The tourist information office also offered public Internet access for the incredibly reasonable price of CHF 3 per hour with the first 20 minutes free (most places charge CHF 12-15 per hour), so we spent an hour handling e-mail.

Then we walked the 1½ miles north to a small commercial campground to pitch our tents. The facilities were nothing short of sparkling: beautiful toilets, sinks, laundry and washing facilities – truly amazing. After a week of either camping rough or having private rooms in small hotels, being lined up in a row of tents, camping trailers and RVs was a big change.

This was our first experience with the system of "menu pricing" at public campsites in Switzerland. Over the next 8 weeks, we were to see charges per tent (often different amounts depending on the size tent and/or the desirability of the tent's location), per person (both to use the facilities and for the local tourist taxes), per 2 minutes of hot water in the shower (a 1 franc coin plunked into the shower automat while you stood gasping under the sudden stream of ice cold water waiting for it to warm up), and per bag of garbage disposed (a different price for each size of bag). If we'd been using the campsite's electricity or water hook-ups, there would have been still more price options.

Since Altdorf is "the crossroads of Switzerland," the other guests at the campground were an eclectic lot. For a while before dinner I wandered up and down the rows comparing notes with the Brits and showing off to the Dutch and the Germans my ability to speak their languages. Within a few minutes I was usually able to tell which country someone was from before hearing them speak, just by looking at their sleeping facilities. The Brits all had huge, three-compartment tents, the Dutch had nearly identical camping trailers, and the Germans and Swiss had pristine, elaborate RVs.

Later, David and Angela sat at one of the tables in front of the campsite's tiny snack bar and ate bratwurst and drank beer while I heated up a greasy sausage in a pot of greasier chicken-noodle soup.

Speaking of crossroads, the night was not particularly restful. Our tents were pitched on the other side of a wooden fence from a major road; a few hundred yards further was the autobahn heading up the Gotthard Pass, and in between was one of the main train lines connecting northern and southern Europe. After midnight the traffic wasn't regular enough to produce the kind of "white" noise that I could sleep through, so I was awakened every few minutes as cars, trucks and trains came roaring past.

By the time I got out of my tent at 6:30 the next morning, the exodus from the campsite was well under way. The Dutch were the first to go, followed by the Brits and then the Germans. By 7:30 we were about the only non-permanent residents left. Clearly, this was not a campsite where people came to stay for days to relax and enjoy nature and peace and quiet.

By the way, "permanent residents" in European campsite terms refers to people with trailers that they leave at the campsite full time. Many of the trailers are set on permanent foundations and have built-in extensions. Some are even surrounded by flower and vegetable gardens inside of little white picket fences.

Rover, Wanderer, Nomad, Vagabond

David   June 30th

And the earth becomes my throne
I adapt to the unknown
Under wandering stars I've grown
By myself but not alone
I ask no one

Rover, wanderer, nomad, vagabond
Call me what you will
- Metallica

There's an old joke in Texas: if your house is on wheels and your car is on bricks, you might be a redneck. Describing the trailers on permanent foundations could evoke a not too dissimilar image – one might imagine broken down pickup trucks, old tires being used as planters, and nonfunctioning washing machines in the front yard for the children to play with.

Rest assured, this trailer park was nothing like that. Later on in the trip we would become quite familiar with weekend campers, families "roughing it up" in their RVs with built-in showers, electric stoves, and DVD players. All these residents fell into that category, except they'd leave the RV there permanently and just drive down from the city for their weekend in the country.

In the morning we left Altdorf and headed up toward the Surenenpass on our way to Engleberg. My mind had definitely made the shift out of city mode. I realized that morning I hadn't seen a newspaper in over a week, so the Western Hemisphere could have fallen off the face of the earth and I wouldn't have known. Nor would I have cared.

I spent the entire day thinking about what it would be like to live my entire life here, a nomad wandering through the Alps, the Pyrenees, the Rhine, the Rhone, and camping day to day, night to night, spending maybe $10 a day on food as I hung out in the middle of nowhere and just ... lived!

In the winters maybe I'd walk to a warmer climate and get a job for a few months, just so I could save up enough money to spend my summers in the absolute freedom of the trees, the mountains, the grass, and the sky. Each year I'd take the time to learn another language, and then live immersed in that language and its culture: French, German, Italian, Dutch, Turkish, Hebrew, Arabic, Portuguese, Norwegian ... . Work one year on a farm, the next as a translator or in the business world, making use of my knowledge of the American language, culture, or industry, and of my experience there and throughout Europe.

There would be women. Likely, they would fall in love with me, and there would be the temptation to stay ... to be with them, to make them happy, to live my life for them. But always, it would come back to this – staring at a backdrop of green fields, mile after mile of knolls and hills, curving upward to insurmountable peaks, or down into snow, which turns into a stream, into a creek, into a river, into a lake; trails cutting through the mountainside, clouds obscuring the view momentarily as they grow, stop, change form, and move on. Always a gentle haze, painting the backdrop like a canvas, making the view look almost fake, like any minute we might turn and run straight into a wall that makes the background on a film set. Off in the distance, peaks cloaked in snow, even now, at the end of June, with the odd glimpse of brown, gray, or green sneaking out from under the white blanket.

(Note from Don: Before we sent this to be published, I begged David to put something in here to make it evident that he knows how ridiculous this all is. "There would be women?" Come on ... . He refused, claiming to be a sex magnet and arguing that this was a totally realistic vision.)

When we reached the top of the Surenenpass, the fog on the side from which we'd come was so thick we saw nothing but white. Turn around and face west, and the sky was completely clear and the view was perfect for miles and miles.

We sat at the top of the pass for a good half hour, basking in the joy of having reached the top. Some cyclists, lying in the grass next to their mountain bikes, greeted us as we reached the summit and were still there when we left. Again, we were miles from anything we considered remotely cyclable, so perhaps they'd just been dropped in by helicopter to psych people out.

As we sat munching trail mix and staring out at the view, a man arrived with a dog that looked like a mix between a German Shepherd and a fox. The dog walked on a few feet to a snow bank, lay down and started rolling around, chomping on the snow as he crawled through it to cool off, all the while smiling at the joy of this life.

Shortly after we started our descent, we came to a gate where we found awaiting us a cow, which, according to Angela, had been mooing in a distressed tone. The cow had spent the last half hour trying to follow hikers up the trail, but kept getting stopped at the gate, which presumably had been put there for precisely that purpose. Seeing her brethren (and sistren) grazing in the valley half a mile below, we decided to usher her down the trail to join them.

At first it was easy. She followed Dad down toward a small hut, licking every bit of exposed skin she could find. When Dad made it clear that he was not interested in a lasting relationship, the cow switched its attentions to me and started licking all over my groin area. (I *told* you there would be women!) While we all conceded that it was an interesting proposition, Angela is not into threesomes, so I had to put a stop to it.

We tried to convince the cow to continue with us down the path to join her colleagues, but she decided she'd rather be a mountain walker and stayed by the hut to graze. Angela tried desperately to lure her on, but to no avail. We eventually decided she knew where all the other cows were and how to get to them, but had been ostracized for some reason and wasn't allowed to go back. We named her Jar-Jar, and as we left her behind, she mooed after us longingly, but refused to follow. A few minutes after continuing our descent, we heard her mooing and looked back to see her once again standing at the gate, staring longingly at the top of the pass.

Hip to Hip in a Mountain Hut

Don   June 30th-July 1st

At the tourist information office in Altdorf the day before, we had gotten a brochure listing accommodations in the area. The brochure included an entry for a mountain hut at Blackenalp on the trail leading down from the Surenenpass. We had heard a lot about Swiss mountain huts and were anxious to try one. But where the entries for all the other mountain huts had prices, there were none listed for Blackenalp. Not a good sign, we concluded. This was Switzerland, where they understand the concept of pricing to what the market will bear. A Big Mac costs $10! Blackenalp is in the middle of nowhere, a 6-hour walk from civilization in one direction and a 3-hour walk in the other. If you get there at sundown and have no alternative, you might end up having to trade a kidney for a place to sleep and a meal.

Consequently, as we walked down from the pass, we started looking for suitable places to pitch our tents. We weren't having much luck, since we were again in intense cow territory, and every place that was not at a 45° angle was covered with cow shit. As we came around a bend in the road, suddenly we were confronted with the Blackenalp Mountain Hut, a large house with a number of tables out front and a sign saying that they offered *Ürbernachtung mit Früstück* (overnight accommodation with breakfast). I went inside to ask the hostess how much it would cost, and was shocked and delighted to be informed that it was only 20 francs per person per night.

We would be staying in the *Massenlager*, which translates literally as "group camp" but more loosely as "Lay-em-down so their hips are touching." Indeed, our hostess showed us upstairs where there were two rooms, each with twelve beds, six on each side of the room. Each side had a twenty-foot-long plank with pads, duvets and pillows lined up – the feet toward the center aisle and the pillows against the walls. Actually, it was very neat and clean and comfortable. A clothesline ran down the middle of the room, which gave us the idea of doing our laundry in the sinks next to the toilet room out in the hall. Since there were no showers, we also used the sinks to give ourselves "executive showers." In Angela's case, that meant wiping herself down with a damp washcloth; in David's and my cases it meant splashing ourselves with the ice-cold water from the tap while we gasped for air and tried to keep our testicles from shrinking to the size of peas.

When we had arrived at around 4 pm, there was only one other occupant in the two rooms, but over the next 2½ hours hikers streamed in steadily. We had not yet decided whether we would buy dinner or cook our own food out in the front yard. But while we lay in our bunks, writing letters and journals and listening to the rushing stream outside the window, the heady aroma of sautéing onions wafting up from the kitchen became overpowering.

Suddenly at 7 pm, as though by some signal that everyone else recognized but we were not party to, both rooms emptied as their occupants trooped down the stairs to the dining room. We followed, only to learn from our hostess that if we had wanted to have dinner we were supposed to have told her when we arrived. Not to worry though, she told us, and she quickly redistributed the contents of 16 bowls of applesauce into 19 bowls. At first we were a little embarrassed to be taking other people's food, but when she appeared with a gigantic wok a foot deep and 3 feet in diameter filled to the brim, it was clear that there would be enough for everyone. The meal was *Älpler magroni*, a traditional mountain dish made with macaroni and potatoes, mixed with lots of sautéed onions and a few pieces of bacon and covered with cheese. Our 16 fellow hikers were as hungry as we were. Everyone finished their first helping in about 3 minutes, and then enthusiastically accepted seconds and whatever else was available as our hostess scraped the wok clean.

Our eight table companions were all Swiss, and they started out keeping pretty much to themselves. However, a few beers loosened things up, and before long we were all chatting enthusiastically about our long trek, marriage, work, retirement, you name it. Occasionally someone would say a few words in English, but for the most part we spoke in German. Angela speaks some German, although she is not nearly as willing to dive in and make mistakes as I am. And David, who does not speak German, was starting to claim that he could understand everything I was saying. He said there are only so many times you can hear "Where did you start?" "Sargans." "Where are you going?" "Mont Blanc." "!!!!!!" before you start to understand it. I couldn't help feeling there was a message there somewhere.

Meanwhile, the hostess sprinted back and forth from the kitchen with trays of beer and schnapps, detouring only to avoid a huge bear of a dog that was blocking nearly all of the floor that was not taken up by tables and chairs and tipsy diners. He looked to be a St. Bernard, Newfoundland cross, and must have weighed over 250 pounds. During the 2 hours we were in the dining room he barely moved. I'm not sure he was able to, but nobody was going to take the chance of annoying our pretty, young hostess to find out.

By the time we got back upstairs, all but two of the 24 Massenlager bunks were full. Several young Greek men had shown up after 8 pm and the proprietress was frying up another pan of Älpler magroni for them. Shortly before I fell asleep, one of the Swiss men came over to my bunk to show me a map with the trails for the next day's walk. Several of our tablemates had told us it was a lovely walk, and there would be lots of cable cars to ease the way. The Swiss don't seem to feel that taking cable cars for major up- and down-hill sections is cheating. More like taking reasonable advantage of an available convenience. There's more than enough altitude to be gained and lost in places where no cable car is available.

In case you hadn't realized it already, Massenlagers are not designed for privacy. There was only one other woman besides Angela among the guests, a cute young Swiss woman three bunks over from me. As I was assembling my gear the next morning, I got a swell view of her changing her clothes, inadequately hidden by a blanket. I discretely averted my eyes. (OK, I only pretended to discretely avert my eyes.) Adequate compensation for a week of walking and camping in the pouring rain? I'll have to think about that and get back to you.

Before we left Blackenalp, I asked the proprietress how they managed to get food supplies to such an isolated place. She said that once a year they have the staples brought in by helicopter. Then, every other week, they have additional supplies sent up from the town on the nearest cable car. They send a small ATV down the footpath to pick them up. On the way back, they have to unload the ATV and carry it and the goods by hand over rocky stretches and stiles five times. The hut is only open from mid-June through mid-September, but they seem to do a great business during those months.

I told her about our trek on the Via Alpina, and she said she'd never heard of it. I pointed out that it goes right past her front door and that there is a Via Alpina trail sign on the other side of the picnic tables in front of the hut. As cosmopolitan as the city Swiss are, the country/mountain Swiss seem to have their vision restricted to their own valley.

Speaking of valleys, every valley in Switzerland has its own distinctive cheese. For lunch each day that we were near a store, we would buy a loaf of bread and a hunk of the local cheese. During my conversation with our hostess in Blackenalp, she proudly informed me that she had made the cheese we had been served for breakfast that morning. It had a wonderful woody aroma and a slightly salty tang. As we walked down the hill from Blackenalp, David and Angela and I agreed that eating the home-made local foods was one of the highlights of our trek.

A short epilogue to our stay in Blackenalp. By that afternoon, I had a ring of welts around my navel, apparently from the bite of some insects in the mattresses or blankets in the Massenlager. Over the next few days, the welts got bigger and bigger, and I suspected that something was breeding in there. I expected that at any moment the monster from the movie *Alien* would come bursting out of my stomach. It was fully 2 weeks before the welts subsided.

Alphütte Ninja Monk

David   July 1st

Blackenalp is named for the red-stemmed leafy greens that cover its
landscape – known as Swiss chard in the States, and Blacken in
Switzerland. Angela was the one who asked what they were called,
since her parents grow it on their farm and used to force her and her
siblings to eat it when they were little. She always hated it, because
of the terribly bitter flavor, and when telling this to the local she'd
asked, he gave her a mystified look and said, "Really? People grow
that? Here, even the cows don't eat it. I always thought it was a
poisonous weed."

After dinner I jumped straight into bed, despite the protests of
Angela, who wanted to explore the farm and pet the horse. It was
only 8:00, but I was so exhausted from the day that I was asleep
almost instantly and remained unconscious for the next 12 hours,
when I woke up lying next to a strange man who hadn't been there
when I went to sleep.
    After leaving Blackenalp, I spent the rest of the morning
fantasizing about making my life running an *Alphütte* (an alpine hut
for hikers, pronounced ALP-hoot-uh) … . Spend the winters in the
valley, breeding the cattle and making cheese. Then in the spring,
bring the herd up into the mountains somewhere, churn butter daily
and mak homemade chocolate milk. Grow wheat so I could make
my own bread, and then make dinner for all the locals and the
tourists passing through. Speak German, English, French … and
maybe learn other languages that seemed useful or essential as time
went on. I thought I could be perfectly happy making a life there.
Either that or I would be perfectly happy dreaming about making a

life there. Hmm.

Late in the morning we reached Einwäldi, which had a grocery store (open on Sunday – unheard of in rural Switzerland!). There we purchased fresh produce, which was something we carefully restricted to times when we weren't planning on going very far between shopping and consumption. In this case it was about 12 yards from the store to a suitable bench.

From there we went on to Engleberg, home of a famous Benedictine monastery and a ski resort that was disgustingly touristy. We realized, it being July 1st, that the summer walking season had officially started, and since it was a Sunday to boot, we marveled at all the old women and nuns out with their walking poles.

Incidentally, I can't express to you the excitement I felt at discovering that everyone called the monastery a cloister. Of course it makes sense, since the German word is *Kloster*; but I was excited because I'm a board game geek, and in the German board game Carcassonne you place your meeples on cloisters – **not** monasteries. In order to indicate your meeple is a monk, you stand him on his head, so I tried to spot the monks at the Engleberg cloister by looking for the people standing on their heads wearing long black robes. I didn't find any, which I must admit was a little disappointing. In Carcassonne you always take the cloister if you can. The Swiss must be lousy at that game.

We stuck around to watch some non-monk employees make *Klosterkäse* (cloister cheese) in the monastery gift shop, before taking the cable car up to the Trüebsee (like *grüezi*, this is pronounced like you're saying "TROOB-zay" while vomiting). The Trüebsee is a small lake about 200 yards wide and 400 yards long that exists for the sole purpose of touristicular enjoyment, and was doing its job admirably. It was absolutely overrun with people. We considered camping by one of the three Feuerstelle surrounding the lake, but it seemed a little conspicuous, like setting up a tent in Washington Square Park in Manhattan, so we decided to try our luck climbing up to the Jochpass to see if we could find a spot there. We had heard from several sources that it was supposed to storm that night, so we wanted to set up camp before it rained. But when you're in the kind of terrain that ascends 400 yards in an hour's walk, finding a spot to camp is much easier said than done.

I should mention at this point that Angela was not especially happy about making that climb. Although she never would've admitted it, she desperately wanted to take the cable car up those last 400 yards. Dad and I suggested that she take the cable car while he and I walk, but she refused, since that would have made her look like a pussy.

At one point during the climb, we thought we might have found something suitable. I went to investigate, but determined that if (when) it rained, we'd wake up with a stream running through the middle of our tents. Only now I was a few hundred yards removed from the trail, and Dad and Angela were gaining altitude rapidly. Not to be outdone, I began scaling rocks as I veered back toward the trail. A few times I had to toss my walking stick over a boulder and hoist myself up like a ninja, throwing my legs over crumbling boulders and rolling over cliffs. Mostly I just wanted to make myself look sexy for Angela. Mission accomplished.

We reached the Jochpass at about 4:30, which was the time the chairlift stopped running. There was a hotel at the top of the pass, but as much as we'd been spending, I was adamant that we weren't going to stay in a hotel, so instead we looked for an inconspicuous place to camp, which was like trying to camp in Central Park – any places that were inconspicuous at that moment, wouldn't be for long. We found a little shelter underneath some exterior stairs at the top of a chairlift, and were very close to camping there until Dad found something *waaay* better. A few hundred yards down the hill was the base station of another chairlift – this one was closed for the summer – and the place was huge. We could've fit an army battalion in there and then stormed the hotel the next morning. Just when you think you've slept everywhere, along comes this.

Walking into the wide open sanctuary, a few rabbits and birds raced past us like we were in a game of Duck Hunt. Dad set his sleeping bag by the front of the shelter, while Angela and I nestled ours on the concrete launching pad further in, far enough away that we could have some nookie and not have to worry about him. As it happened, between the storm and the altitude, the temperature dropped down near freezing that night, so when I awoke rubbing myself against Angela, I was too cold to get out of my sleeping bag and do anything further about it. But we were dry and we were happy, and that's what was important.

Lizard Love

Don   **July 2nd**

A huge storm blew all that night. We were over 7,000 feet high and it was absolutely frigid, but at least we stayed dry under the cavernous shelter of the ski lift station. David, who tends to be paranoid about these sorts of things, was afraid that there were video surveillance cameras secreted around the structure. This was supported by the fact that the control room of the ski lift was next to where he and Angela had rolled out their sleeping bags; behind a large glass window, we could see red lights flickering ominously throughout the night.

As if David's natural tendencies aren't bad enough, he has been mightily influenced by my tales of Switzerland being a police state. The Swiss have rules for everything, and they are damned serious about them. When the Fried Family first moved to Zurich in 1987, we stayed for 2 months in a small apartment building. On the day we moved in we were given a pamphlet of the building rules, which included not taking showers or flushing toilets after 10 pm. There was also a schedule for using the building washer and dryer; each apartment was allocated exclusive use of the facilities for two entire **consecutive** days in each 2-week period. A few months later, when we moved into our house, Rhonda was harangued by a neighbor because she was mowing the lawn – with an electric lawn mower – between the noon and 2 pm "quiet" hours. And a work colleague of mine was given a ticket for washing his car on a Sunday. A neighbor had called the police to "inform" on him.

While we were living in Zurich there had been a big scandal when it was revealed that the Swiss national intelligence organization was actively spying and had secret files on a large percentage (40%?) of the population of the country. When we'd arrived 2 weeks earlier I had asked Elena and Tomas about what the outcome of the scandal had been. They said they expected that now, 20 years later, the figure was more in the 60% range.

When I was in Zurich on business in 1991, I heard a story on the radio of an American reporter who periodically came to Geneva to cover activities at the United Nations office there. On one trip, in the middle of his first night in the country he was awakened by the local police banging on his hotel room door. They seized him and took him to jail – **in his underwear**! Clearly whatever he had done was far too dangerous to allow him to get dressed. The next morning, he was informed that several years earlier he had rented a car and gotten a parking ticket, which there was no record of him having paid. When you check into a Swiss hotel you have to fill out a police registration form, and when this unfortunate soul's form had been keyed into the system the night before, alarm bells had started ringing all over the country. Fortunately for him he had, in fact, paid the ticket and, knowing the Swiss national mentality, he'd had the foresight to save the receipt. Unfortunately for him, the receipt was in New York, and it was most of a day before he could get a copy of it sent to the Geneva police and gain his release.

Coincidentally, on the same trip on which I'd heard that story I had rented a car and gotten a parking ticket. I kept the receipt and carried it with me every time I went to Switzerland until we left Europe in 2004. I didn't have it with me during our trek, which worried me more than a little.

Having been brought up on these and dozens of similar stories, David was terrified that some time during the night units of some elite Swiss military or civil law enforcement agency (The Swiss Coast Guard? The Ski-lift Police?) were going to rappel down from hovering helicopters, storm the lift station, and cart us off to a secret prison deep under the streets of Bern from which we would never emerge. Or at least they'd expel us from our dry, sheltered ski lift to wander endlessly through the sleet and freezing fog at the top of the Jochpass. But I guess whoever's job it was to come kick us out wasn't any more interested in braving the storm than we were, because we made it through the night unevicted.

"... and He made them wander in the desert forty years ..."

I was first out of my sleeping bag the next morning, and discretely kept my eyes averted (I seem to have to do that a lot) from the other side of the ski lift from where David and Angela's sleeping bags were making suspicious rustling noises. Why anybody would want to risk exposing bare skin in conditions like that was beyond me. But I guess that's the difference between being 25 and being 55.

(Note from David: In all fairness, any time Angela and I wanted to make suspicious rustling noises, we watched Dad for several minutes to make sure he was sleeping, or possibly frozen to death. More often than not, we rustled about pumping ourselves up to leave the coziness of our sleeping bags.)

We had only enough water left for cooking and drinking, and although there were snow-patches on the mountain slope a few hundred yards away, I wasn't in any mood to bundle up and go out into the storm before it was absolutely necessary. So after breakfast I washed the dishes under the drip of rainwater at the edge of the roof where the ski-cable stopped its downward trajectory and leveled off. It took a while, but it wasn't as though I had anything else important to do.

As we left the shelter of the lift station and headed down from the pass in full rain gear, the weather alternated between cold/windy/drizzling and cold/windy/pouring rain. A few minutes after starting, we came upon what looked to be a shiny black plastic toy sitting in the middle of the trail. I bent down to take a closer look, and it moved, albeit at glacial speed. It looked like a lizard, about 5 inches long, and fantastically ugly, like something from the dinosaur age. Over the next hour, we came upon thousands more. The lone ones were mostly basking in the damp on the exposed trail. If we approached one or prodded it with a stick, it would recoil a bit and then sprint off at the lightning pace of a step every 3 or 4 seconds. I guess the lone ones were the least attractive, because most of them were paired up and engaging in what looked remarkably like human missionary-position copulation. What is it with this mountain air? First Angela and David, and now a mountain-wide lizard orgy.

David said that lizards only live in hot, dry climates and that we should call them salamanders. Further research would prove that they were actually Alpine Newts, of the species *Mesotriton alpestris*. But Salamander Love, Newt Love, and *Mesotriton alpestris* Love don't trip off the tongue quite like Lizard Love.

As we continued down the mountain, David and I speculated on how a species that slow and apparently unprotected could survive.

Perhaps it's simply their numbers. That much lizard-love is bound to produce a lot of little lizards. Perhaps they are poisonous. They certainly didn't look appetizing to me, but then I'm not a bearded alpine vulture, and none of us was willing to lick one to find out. Maybe the lizards are not indigenous at all, but the advance team from an alien planet sent to soften us up for the impending invasion of earth, and their bigger cousins would be along shortly. (I know the paranoia of that last one sounds like David, but I was the one who came up with it.)

We walked downhill for over 7 hours, at times through gentle valleys, and at times along narrow paths set into the sides of precipitous cliffs. The rain had made the path, especially the rocks and roots, particularly treacherous, and I slipped and nearly fell several times. I'm not afraid of heights, but I was certainly glad when we left the cliff-side and were back walking through farms. Once again, David and Angela castigated me for walking ahead of them. I suppose after all the times I'd told them about my vast experience walking in the mountains, if I was going to go plummeting to my death they wanted to be there to enjoy it. *(Note from David: Yes, Dad was not shy about taking every opportunity to remind us how many more miles he has in the footbank than we do. The result was that Angela's reaction whenever Dad slipped on a rock was, "Take that, footbank!")* Our only respite from the rain was when we stopped at a farm to buy cheese for lunch and sat for a half hour on a bench in front of their barn while we ate.

Finally, we slogged into the splendid town of Meiringen, at the west end of the Briensersee (at the other end of which is Interlaken). Meiringen is flanked to the east, south and southwest by the Sustenenpass, the Grimselpass, and Grosse Scheidegg, which are some of the highest road passes in Switzerland and are drivable only from late spring to early autumn. When Rhonda and I first came to Switzerland in 1974, we tried to drive over the Grimselpass during the first week of September. We couldn't make it over the top and had to back down the mountain in the dark and in deep snow until we got to a place where we could turn our car around.

Meiringen was made famous by Arthur Conan Doyle, who used it as the setting for Sherlock Holmes' "first" death in *The Final Case*. Although the first Sherlock Holmes stories had appeared only 2 years earlier in 1891, they immediately became wildly successful and by 1893 Doyle had published 24 of them. By that time, however, Doyle had tired of the pressure to churn out what he considered to be pulp fiction and wanted to free himself to produce more lofty historical novels and non-fiction works. He decided to kill off Holmes and his arch-nemesis Professor Moriarty by sending them plunging to their deaths over the Reichenbach Falls (just above

Meiringen) during a titanic hand-to-hand struggle. However, Doyle hadn't counted on the public's attachment to Holmes. Londoners dressed in mourning and letters flooded in, some accusing Doyle of brutality. So during 1901 and 1902 he wrote the *Hound of the Baskervilles* recounting a number of adventures which had taken place before Holmes' death. Still, the public outcry at Holmes' death continued, and by 1903 Doyle capitulated and resurrected the master detective in *The Adventure of the Empty House*. It seems that Holmes had faked his own death to avoid continued pursuit by Moriarty's henchman.

Meiringen enthusiastically capitalizes on its association with Sherlock Holmes, but manages to do so in a non-tacky way. Sure, there's a Sherlock Holmes Museum, a Sherlock Holmes Hotel, and numerous statues and information signs, but they are all well presented and many of the houses in the town are surrounded by magnificent flower gardens which gives much of the place an up-market, Victorian feel.

By the way, Meiringen also claims to be the source of the word "meringue," although there doesn't seem to be any linguistic evidence to support that claim. By all accounts its origin is in the French language, though that's as far as any dictionary is willing to venture an etymological history.

It was still raining when we arrived, and even if it hadn't been, after seven sodden hours of walking we were ready for a roof and a shower. We stopped at the tourist information office, which made reservations for us at a nearby hostel. When we arrived at the hostel 10 minutes later, we were shocked to see what seemed like 50 screaming 13 year olds, French- and German-speaking Swiss on school trips. It was 4 o'clock and we weren't allowed to check-in until 5, so we made use of the two crude showers in the basement entrance "shoe" hall, washed our clothes in cold water in the utility sink, and hung them up in the games room, which had 10 clotheslines strung across the ceiling. All during the process, kids would open the door to the games room, see us and the clothes hanging everywhere, freak out, and leave.

We were concerned that we would have to sleep in a dormitory room with the kids, but it turned out that we had a four-bunk room for the three of us. We went out for dinner and came back at 8 pm to the continual screaming and thumping of the kids as they raced up and down the halls and stairs. At 10 pm, though, their chaperones announced that it was quiet time, and within a few minutes the hostel had fallen completely silent. The Swiss and their rules. I love it.

Grosse What?

David   July 3rd-4th

We spent the next day climbing from Meiringen to Grosse Scheidegg – a 5 hour journey that actually took us just about 5 hours, cause for celebration considering the hell we'd gone through clawing our way over the Foopass 2 weeks earlier.

Along the way we had another run-in with overly-affectionate cattle. No sooner had we walked through a gate before an entire herd of calves stampeded toward us and began licking our backpacks with every step. Every so often I'd stop and turn around to pet one, and it would lick my hand or my arm or my crotch or whatever else it could get close to, always with a disappointed look on its face. That experience taught me that it doesn't matter what species it is, when someone looks disappointed with your crotch, it still deals a serious blow to your self-esteem.

After about 15 minutes of this, we crossed paths with a pair of farmers, and all was revealed. Obviously bemused by our situation at the center of the herd, they reached into little sacks on their belts and started throwing handfuls of salt onto the ground. The calves, who had apparently mistaken us for their daily salt truck, suddenly lost interest in us completely and began crowding around the two men who obviously had what they wanted and began licking the salted ground furiously. Now I'll know to carry salt with me for the next time I get propositioned by an eligible young bovine.

Inspired by a sign for the Rösti[7] special, we stopped at a roadside

---

[7] Rösti is one of the Swiss national dishes. A big hash brown patty with bacon or ham, covered with cheese, baked in a casserole with an egg on top.

restaurant for lunch, where Dad, exhausted and not thinking straight, made a rather inappropriate slip of the tongue.[8] We were talking about how Mom grew up cooking for her family of six, so when she and Dad first got married (and she continued cooking for six) he gained 25 lbs, which he never lost, but "grew into." I told Angela, "That's the trick," meaning, if she wants to fatten me up, to cook for 6, but Dad's ill-thought-out reply to her was "That's right, you'd be the perfect weight if you were 6'4".

The table fell silent. I'm not an expert in the female mind, but I had a feeling that this was not a bright thing for him to have said. I made a joke of the situation, but in reality, there are only two things you can do in a situation like this: (1) run away, or (2) act like you just got caught with your pants down, pretend nothing happened, and ultimately suffer the impact of a well-planned and highly humiliating revenge attack. *(Feeble attempt at defense by Don: I thought they were making similar cracks and it just slipped out. I knew immediately that it was a relationship-terminating comment. Mea culpa.)*

Angela, to her credit, never mentioned the event again. Dad recently asked me whether that means she's forgiven him, but I think it's more likely that she's just repressed the memory and is still plotting her revenge. In fact, only a couple of hours later as we passed an incredibly scenic rock bluff surrounded by clouds on all sides, Angela and I discussed what we could do to thank him for making this entire trip possible. We both became very emotional, realizing that this is the stuff Thanksgivings are made of. Okay, I became very emotional. Angela laughed at me for crying like a little

---

[8] That reminds me of one of my favorite jokes: Two guys are sitting next to each other on a flight to Pittsburgh, each with a black eye. One asks the other how he got his black eye, to which the response was: "Oh, it was a slip of the tongue. This morning when I got to the airport the lady at the ticket counter was very busty, and I meant to say, 'Can I have a ticket to Pittsburgh?' but what came out is 'Can I have a picket to Titsburgh?' And she socked me one right in the eye." The other guy replied, "Oh, mine was a slip of the tongue, too. This morning as I was walking into the kitchen I meant to say to my wife, "Hi, honey, what's for breakfast?" and instead what came out was, "You ruined my life, you bitch!"

girl. (*Note from Angela: (a) I will never forget, and am still plotting my revenge, and (b) David teared up at a mountain! What on earth was I marrying into?!*)

Just Another Tearjerking View

By the time we reached the top of the pass the clouds were so thick we could barely see the hotel a few yards in front of us. As we ate dinner that evening, the hotel was completely shrouded in white on all sides – we couldn't even see the garden furniture 3 feet outside our window. This provided for some rather chummy exchanges with our waitress (we jokingly asked her if we could sit outside to eat, and she just laughed and laughed and laughed), but things got sour a little while later. Angela and Dad tried letting me order dessert in German, *ein Apfelstrudel mit drei Gabel* (an apple strudel with three forks). They thought I did very well, but when the waitress brought us three coffees (apparently *Gabel* sounded to her like *Café*) we wondered if maybe my ordering hadn't been such a good idea. We sent the coffees back, so to get back at us she charged us a dollar a glass for our tap water.

Of course, charging for tap water is a common practice in much of Europe, and all three of us knew that. But this was the first, and would prove to be the only time in the entire trip that this happened. When we complained to our waitress, she argued with us: "This is very common practice in Europe; I used to wait tables in Brussels and we did it there." Dad spent 5 days a week in Brussels for a year and a half, and knew perfectly well that you get charged for tap water there, but as he so accurately pointed out to our waitress, we weren't in Brussels just at the moment.

No matter. We slept in a Massenlager that night, but this time it was just the three of us in a room with 11 beds in it. A storm pounded on our roof all night, and as we drifted to sleep, thunder rolled in the distance, and the force of the wind made the windows clatter and the building creak like a ship.

In the morning we bundled up, grabbed our equipment, and stood by the entrance, psyching ourselves up for the day. By the time we stepped outside the wind must have been 40 mph and it was sleeting sideways. As Dad started toward the trail, Angela and I made a beeline for a tour bus that had serendipitously arrived just as we were leaving. When Dad turned around and realized we were nowhere to be found, he put two and two together very quickly and followed us to the bus, where we agreed to the extortionate 20 francs per person fare to take us the 20-minute ride down to Grindelwald.

As we sat there, our backpacks in our laps, sharing a bus with a large group of Japanese tourists, a part of me felt some regret at having missed the adventure and dropping that kind of money for a trip down the mountain, particularly when the weather cleared up almost immediately once we descended a few feet. But as miserable as those long, steep downhill climbs are – especially when your toe is sore (and mine was – I'd had blisters on both pinky toes ever since Altdorf) – I quickly got over my lament.

It was barely drizzling by the time we got off the bus in Grindelwald, so we removed all our raingear, only to have the rain start up again a few minutes later. We held off as long as we could – taking shelter, walking through it, trying to bend over so our backpacks would protect our legs and torsos from getting wet. But soon we had to relent, and put on all our rain gear for the walk to Lauterbrunnen.

We had discovered that morning that the Via Alpina actually took a long and difficult route in the shadows of the Eiger and the Jungfrau over the pass to Kleine Scheidegg, a 4½-hour trek in its own right, followed by 2-2½ hours down into Lauterbrunnen. But with the weather as threatening as it was, and as much climbing as we'd already done, we were much happier taking the valley around, which was a mere 4 hours of more or less level terrain along two rivers.

As we walked toward Lütschintal en route to the valley intersection of Zweilütschinen, the rain stopped. By this time we were extremely superstitious, convinced that any attempt we made at removing our rain gear would be a direct affront to the weather gods, and that they'd smite us with thunder almost immediately. We spent the rest of the morning playing games and trying to outsmart them. Dad took his rain pants off, but left his jacket on. I removed my jacket and my fleece, but kept my rain pants on, "taking one for the team."

A glimmer of blue sky opened up in the narrow valley before us and started to shine down on us just a little stronger. We stopped to apply sunscreen – Dad and I only to the back of our necks and ears, since the sun couldn't possibly last long enough for us to need sunscreen anywhere else.

We passed a "Self-service Alpkäse and Bier" barn – a little fridge where you could grab a beer, some cheese, mineral water, or butter, and drop the requisite money into the coin slot below, all on the honor system. Dad said, "We're not in Kansas anymore, Toto." I allowed as how you could probably do the same thing in Kansas, although perhaps without the beer. Or, for that matter, the mountains.

We happened upon a British couple who walked with us a little way. They had stopped to look at a bird they'd spotted, and since we were walking in the same direction, we continued on together and chatted about life in England and our various experiences. I got the impression they wanted to be by themselves, and after a few moments they found an excuse to break off the path from us, and we continued on our way.

With the sky continuing to clear up in front of us, I took off my rain pants (bad move) and the bottom half of my pants (the legs had zippers on them so they could be converted into shorts) and tied them onto my backpack as we continued on.

Finally, around 1:00 we stopped for lunch. Included on the menu was some extra cheese we'd picked up at breakfast that morning. (The chef had come to our table and asked us if we wanted anything else, and though we were full, he looked us with an expression of such anxiety and expectation, we couldn't bear the thought of hurting his feelings.)

And then, from out of nowhere, the temperature dropped, the wind began screaming, and the sky turned black. A few minutes later, it felt like the sky was falling in. The rain poured down for mile after mile, dripping off our clothes and our packs and soaking through both. I drew my hood in tight and trudged on, hunched over, with my hands in my pockets, looking up every now and then to make sure I could still see Dad off in the distance ahead of us.

By the time we made it to Zweilütschinen, I was so fed up with the rain I was about ready to hop on the next train to Geneva or Zurich or Rome or New York or somewhere else where I wouldn't have to put up with the miserable [expletive deleted] weather.

Incidentally, *Lütschen* is German for "to suck," which means that presumably Zweilütschinen means "two sucky places." Later, when we asked Elena and Tomas about it, they told us that Lütschin is the name of a pair of rivers – that there is a Black Lütschin and a White Lütschin, and that Lütschintal is "Valley of the Lütschin," and Zweilütschinen is where the two Lütschins come together.

I like our explanation better – as we walked from one to the other, the whole thing sucked pretty badly. I was thoroughly pissed off, shuffling my feet, kicking pebbles, picking up large rocks and throwing them into the river, which was now galloping in the opposite direction from our travel.

About half an hour outside Lauterbrunnen we came to a

Feuerstelle next to a small cave-like tower where we decided to take shelter for a few moments. Looking up at the dripping ceiling a few inches above our heads we could see the tiny settlings of mineral deposits beginning to form, a few millimeters to a few inches in length. It was cool to realize we were witnessing the formation of stalactites – a few hundred years in the making, rather than hundreds of thousands.

A few minutes later we left our shelter, the rained slowed to a drizzle, and we climbed up the hill and into Lauterbrunnen.

Yanks to Left of Them, Brits to Right of Them

Don   **July 4ᵗʰ-5ᵗʰ**

Lauterbrunnen

Grindelwald and Lauterbrunnen have been popular tourist destinations, in particular with people from the English-speaking world, for the past 130 years. Many of the street and store signs are in English; there are hotels named Victoria, Derby, and Park Royal; and there's a restaurant named Uncle Tom's Cottage. Whatever they've been doing, it was clearly working. Lauterbrunnen was bustling with tourists as we slogged up the final hill into the town. The first week of our trek we rarely came across any Anglo-Saxons. Sometimes people would know how to speak English, but their first approach was always made in Swiss German. If that approach was to David, his eyebrows would pucker in panic and his head would whip around to see if I was close enough to rescue him. In Lauterbrunnen, we were usually greeted in English when we walked into a store, and on the street we heard more English being spoken than German.

Our first stop was the tourist office. We asked about campgrounds and were informed that the two campgrounds in town were full. We looked at each other in astonishment. It had been raining nearly every day for the past month and although it was only drizzling at that moment, it had been pouring for most of the day. And the campgrounds were full! I guess there's no accounting for some people's idea of fun. On the other hand, the occupants of the campgrounds were undoubtedly doing the same thing we were – trying to avoid paying upwards of $100 per person per night for a hotel room. We negotiated prices briefly with the girl behind the desk, and she quickly realized that $300 a night was not what we were looking for. Then she told us about a "basic" hotel that was charging about $25 a night per person and might still have a room available. Frantic to get there before the last room was gone, we hoisted our packs and hustled up the main street and around a corner to find a wonderful, ramshackle old building with rooms in every direction.

Our room was a huge, four-bedded affair with a dining table. First we made use of our first free hot water in a week to do our laundry. In what was to become a familiar ritual over the next 6 weeks, we started by trying to string a clothesline between two chairs, but the weight of the wet laundry kept pulling the chairs over. Then we looked around for exposed water-pipes, doorknobs, and window handles to which to tie the line. Eventually the room was crisscrossed by low-hanging twine and lower-hanging clothes. And, of course, every time we opened a door or a window, wet t-shirts and socks would go flying onto the beds and the floor. No matter how conscientiously we maintained the proper position when moving around the room – hunched over with back bent, head to the side, eyes nervously scanning the horizon – every few minutes there would be the sound of a wet smack and a muffled curse.

Angela and David went off to a little local grocery store to buy fixings for dinner, which they prepared and cooked on the dining table. Although the rain had tapered off for a few minutes while they were shopping, by the time we finished dinner it had started to pour again. I went down to speak with the hotel manager, and she told me that the forecast for the next day was for more of the same. I told her that it was probably my fault; I seem to bring record precipitation with me wherever I go. During the first 12 months that I lived in Germany in 1974-5, there were 320 days of measurable precipitation. When I moved to San Francisco in 1977, they were on the tail end of a 5-year drought. As soon as I arrived, it started raining and didn't stop for the next 6 months. And I've already told you about the end-to-end walk through Great Britain. The manager replied that she would talk to the local town council to see if they wanted to take up a collection and give me all the money if I would agree to leave.

In any case, Angela, David and I were so thrilled to be warm and dry that we were happy to stay until the weather cleared – especially since the next two stages would be the highest and most exposed of the Via Alpina in Switzerland. When I got out of bed the next morning, I walked down the hall to the balcony at the front of the hotel which looked up the valley toward the south in the direction of our next stage. It was drizzling steadily, and the mountains were completely obscured by clouds. I went back to the room, and after a brief conference, Angela, David and I decided to make that day a true dry-out, sleep in a bed, eat until you explode R&R day.

A while later I went down to the hotel manager's office to extend our stay. She told me that the longer-term forecast was now for gradual improvement. To date the weather forecasts had been pretty accurate. So although Angela, David and I decided not to pawn our rain gear just yet, we were reasonably hopeful.

After breakfast we walked through town to run various errands: take a letter to the post office; buy an *International Herald Tribune* at the train station; check e-mail at an Internet café; get cash at an ATM; do grocery shopping. Since we would again be cooking in the room and wouldn't have to worry about weight, refrigeration, or fragility, we could go hog wild on groceries – things like pork chops, tomatoes and potato chips. You have no idea how good a paprika-flavored potato chip can taste when you've been subsisting mostly on granola, peanut butter and crackers, bread and cheese, and dehydrated mashed potatoes and tuna fish for 2 weeks. By noon we had finished most of a pound bag of chips and a punnet of strawberries; a salad with lettuce, avocados, carrots, tomatoes, shrimp and French dressing; and chicken cordon bleu. Dessert was the omnipresent Lindt chocolate bar. When you are carrying a full pack up and down mountains for 5-8 hours a day, 5-6 days a week, and preparing most of your food from what you are carrying, only the occasional eating orgy like that can set things right.

Angela and David then settled in for a nap while I read the *Herald Trib* from cover to cover. I had glanced at the headlines on German newspapers as we had walked through villages and towns for the past 2 weeks, but other than that I had absolutely no idea what had been going on in the world. It was exciting, reassuring and discomforting to catch up: exciting to see what had been going on; reassuring that the world seemed to be getting along fine without me watching it; and discomforting that the world seemed to be getting along fine without me watching it. I was gratified to find that I could still do the whole *New York Times* crossword puzzle. It will take more than a 2-week hiatus to deprive me of a skill that has taken me 30 years to acquire.

I was also gratified to find that the little butcher shop from which we had bought rotisserie chickens nearly every night when we had rented an apartment in Lauterbrunnen for a week in 1989 was still there and was still making rotisserie chickens. We had one for dinner, and it was as good I remembered.

Before we went to bed we started making plans to get Angela back to Zurich the following Tuesday to catch her plane back to the United States. By Monday morning we'd have to be in a town of sufficient size that it would have either a car rental agency or some kind of public transportation service. By Monday night we'd have to get her to Elena and Tomas's house to pick up her suitcase. Tuesday morning she'd board the plane, and by Tuesday evening David and I would have made our way back across half the country to where we'd left off. Then it would be on into Francophone Switzerland and across the border to France and Mont Blanc.

Death Pass – Part 1

Don   **July 6th**

The next morning dawned overcast and drizzling, but the forecast was for better weather and you should always listen to your weather forecaster. Besides, we had been lounging around in Lauterbrunnen for 36 hours and were starting to get antsy.

The Lauterbrunnen Valley is bordered on its east and west sides by steep mountains; the head of the valley, to the south, is sealed by a massive ridge of mountains including the Jungfrau and the Eiger. Every year hundreds of thousands of tourists come to Lauterbrunnen and Grindelwald to ride the Jungfraubahn, a railway that enters the base and ascends through tunnels inside the two mountains to Jungfraujoch, the highest railway stop in Europe at over 11,300 feet. The Eiger is also famous for its notorious North Face. A nearly vertical 6,000-foot wall, it has claimed the lives of 50 climbers since 1935.

Other than heading north down the valley to Interlaken, the only ways out if you aren't a mountain climber are the way we had come in over the pass from Grosse Scheidegg, or to the southwest over the Sefinenfurgge Pass. Since it would be a long, hard 2-day walk, we decided to make use of the 4-mile, 1,100-yard head-start that the local ski facilities offered by taking the cable car up the side of the mountain and the train along the ridge to Mürren. Mürren is a car-free ski resort situated on a flat spot above Lauterbrunnen. It has world-renowned views of the Jungfrau and the Eiger above, the valley and the White Lütschinen River below, and Wengen, another car-free resort, in a bowl-shaped depression above Lauterbrunnen on the other side of the valley. From Mürren, another cable car goes up to the rotating Piz Gloria Restaurant at the top of Schilthorn. The restaurant featured prominently in the 1969 James Bond movie, *On Her Majesty's Secret Service.*

From Mürren we walked for 3 hours along the side of the ridge toward the massifs to the south, before heading steeply up and over a cliff and into a side canyon to the southwest. We reached the Poggangen mountain hut shortly after a group of Swiss hikers who had passed us a while before. They went into the hut to eat a prepared lunch, while we sat outside in the freezing wind to eat our crackers and peanut butter and jelly and to survey the terrain. The valley floor, which had started out 3,000 feet below, had come up to meet us. And the river, which had been a cascading torrent most of the day, had dwindled into a tiny stream that we could step across with ease. Ahead of us and on both sides, snow-covered mountain walls rose sharply. To get out of that valley, barring some magical twist of the laws of physics, we were going to have to climb over one of those mountain walls. The good news was that it wasn't raining at the moment. At that altitude and temperature, any precipitation probably would have come down as snow anyway.

We've all heard the old adage about the only things certain in life being death and taxes. I'd like to suggest another one. And that is that it takes a lot less time to prepare and eat peanut butter and jelly on crackers when you are freezing your ass off on a windy rock than it does to sit in front of a roaring fire in a mountain hut and eat wienerschnitzel and french fries prepared by a chef. Mind you, I haven't done a rigorous statistical analysis, but the anecdotal evidence is pretty strong. In any case, we finished our meal and headed on up the mountain well in advance of the group of Swiss hikers.

Once more, as had become habit by this time, I would start out walking with David and Angela and some time later realized that I was alone. Then I'd stop anywhere from 5 to 15 minutes until they caught up, and we'd start the process again. One of the times I was waiting, the Swiss hikers came past again.

Trailing in the distance, but closing gradually, was a lone hiker. As the figure got closer, I could see that it was a small woman, probably not much more than 5 feet tall. She was wearing a big floppy hat and an open trench coat that billowed out behind her in the wind. Suspended from a string around her neck was a plastic map case. Over the next hour, each time I stopped to wait for David and Angela, I'd see her approaching and wonder what the hell she was doing up there. Hiking alone at that altitude and that far from the nearest town is never a great idea. You see people doing it occasionally, but not that often. From the way she was walking, taking short, rapid steps and stumbling frequently, I could tell that she was not an experienced mountain hiker. And with her small day pack, she was clearly not equipped to spend the night alone on the mountain if something should go wrong.

But she continued closing the distance between us, hopping along with quick, determined little steps. Suddenly I realized who she must be: a tiny figure in a bizarre costume; hurrying unprepared through the mountains as though on an important mission. She's a hobbit! She's got to get to the Crack of Doom to destroy the Map Case of Power before the Swiss Rule-Masters catch her. *(Note from David: And as Gollum Dad has to stop her.)*[9]

Of course the reality turned out to be a lot less dramatic. An hour later, as I was waiting in the snow underneath the final 1,000-foot cliff leading to the top of the pass, my diminutive pursuer came up and turned out to be a young oriental woman. She stopped briefly to speak with me and it became quickly apparent that if my identification of her as a hobbit was not accurate, at least my assessment of her lack of preparedness for the mountains was. Her name was Wei Wei, and she was a student from China finishing up her BA in economics at Lancaster University in England. (That explained the map case, which is a piece of equipment which is available worldwide, but which I've seen being used almost exclusively in Great Britain. Hers was the only one other than mine that I saw in 9 weeks on the trail.) She was on summer break and had bought a book on hiking in Switzerland. Now, with little

---

[9] Interesting side note: In Hebrew, *golem* means "shapeless mass," and is often translated as "unformed" or "imperfect." According to the Talmud, Adam was considered a "golem," or "body without soul" for the first 12 hours of his existence.

preparation and less equipment, she was walking hut to hut and town to town for 10 days.

We looked up at the cliff above us where several groups of hikers were inching their way up and down the snow-covered trail. She said she was concerned, and I admitted that I was as well. But since there was no meaningful assistance or advice I could give her, after a few minutes she left me to head on toward the summit while I continued to wait for David and Angela.

When they arrived, we set off in our "high-mountain danger formation" – David leading, Angela in the middle, and me at the back. That way, if Angela slipped, she wouldn't have to die alone; she would fall back into me and we would both plummet over the cliff to our deaths. The trail was now mostly covered with snow and slush; if Angela and I hadn't had our trekking poles, our feet would have slipped out from under us on nearly every step.

David, meanwhile, was doing his Tigger imitation, bounding up the trail assisted only by a broken tree branch he had picked up a few days earlier and had become strangely emotionally attached to. More about that stick later.

The footing on the portions of the trail that weren't covered with snow was made up of tiny pieces of black slate, which crumbled into little avalanches beneath our feet with every step we took. If we had lost our footing, we would have tumbled down the 45+° slope for hundreds of yards. In front of me, Angela was absolutely petrified, sometimes frozen in fear, and sometimes sobbing quietly. That kind of fear is contagious, and while I put on a brave face, I was seriously wondering if we were going to make it alive over the top of that pass.

There were three things that convinced me to keep going, though. First was the fact that we could see several groups of hikers moving up ahead of us and disappearing over the top. Still others were heading in the other direction and making their way down towards us. If they had survived it, then so could we! Probably. Maybe? Second was the fact that we had been walking up for nearly 5 hours and were now only a few hundred yards from the top. And third, two of us were men. And real men never turn around, no matter how stupid continuing appears to be.

As it turned out, it took us another hour to make it those last few hundred yards.

Death Pass – Part 2

David   July 6th

There were a couple of times I had to retreat and grab hold of Angela to pull her forward past a rock that jutted out inconveniently into the path. She grew progressively more hysterical. Snot would come halfway down her nose before she'd snort it back, tears streaming down her face. A couple of times she had to stop and consciously slow her breathing to keep from hyperventilating. *(Note from Angela: Snot, yes. Terrified, oh, yeah. You try controlling your emotions when you know that either you, your careless fiancé, or his father are surely going to die. Oh, and Death Pass was my name for it. I'm a genius.)*

When we neared the top of the pass, I went ahead, as I often do in the approach to a landmark, to get a sneak preview and to scope it out. Expecting to be greeted with breathtaking views and a few smiling, satisfied hikers (and cyclists?), I was instead blasted with 30 mph winds and a ridge that was roughly the width of two people. During the climb I had noticed the clouds climbing up over the pass, and I had been looking forward to watching them head toward and over me, but instead I was too afraid to look up for fear of getting blown off the ridge and plummeting backwards to my doom over the cliff I'd just climbed.

It took a few more minutes for Dad and Angela to reach me, and then they too were blasted by the wind. Angela grabbed hold of the signpost that marked the top of the pass and refused to let go. In the meantime, Dad and I looked around for a way down, but we couldn't find one! The trail sign to which Angela so steadfastly clung pointed in three directions: back in the direction from which we had come; along the ridge (a path that looked about as safe as walking along the top of Sears Tower without a safety harness); and directly in front of us, where there was a cable fastened into the shale (with who knows what degree of security) and, after about 15 feet, a dropoff into some unknown abyss.

We stood there like idiots for several minutes. We weren't really supposed to grab onto that cable and abseil down the cliff, were we? Our state of shock was such that we weren't debating our choices so much as wondering whether a helicopter rescue was a legitimate option.

Eventually we saw people climbing up the cliff using the cable, so we figured that must actually be the way to go. In the distance we could see Wei Wei, now apparently with a guide of some kind, halfway down the slope. Being the fearless leader that I am, I agreed to go ahead, scope out the territory, drop my pack down below, and then return to assist Angela with the descent. Dad, meanwhile, would stay back and make sure that Angela didn't lose her grip on the trail sign. (Somehow, I didn't think we had to worry about that. We could've removed her arms at the elbow and she still would've held tight with the stumps she had left.)

After descending a few yards, though, I discovered that it wasn't all that bad – the cable went down for about a quarter of a mile, and for most of it there were steps, which about two dozen people were in the process of climbing up. I returned immediately to share the news with the rest of my party, and we began to assemble our "reverse high-mountain danger formation," with Dad leading the way, and me waiting for Angela to go next, so I could bring up the rear. (The reverse high-mountain danger formation has the same advantage for descents as the high-mountain danger formation has for ascents; Angela would take Dad with her over the cliff if she lost her footing.) Dad grabbed the cable and stepped over the edge. The cinders went sliding out from under his feet and he started sliding down the slope on his back. Fortunately he'd had the foresight to put on gloves, and he squeezed the cable until he managed to skid to a halt in a pile of rubble after about 15 feet. Angela immediately returned to clutching the trail marker pole, and again refused to let go.

By the time I'd managed to pry her away a second time, Dad, naturally had disappeared from view, and it would be another hour or so before we'd catch up to him. In the meantime, I'd stand in place for 5 or 6 minutes while Angela, emitting constant whimpers of panic, would descend 20 yards, after which I'd wrap my wrist around the cable and slingshot myself down as fast as I could, bringing a small avalanche down on top of both of us which invariably comforted Angela immensely.

Eventually the slope leveled out, we made it to more even ground, and Angela was able to calm down enough to consider the magnitude of her accomplishment.

When we finally caught up to Dad, he'd met up again with Wei Wei. Her escort had been a young Finnish man who had been with one of the hiking groups maneuvering their way down the cliff on the other side of the pass. They had come upon a lone and very scared Wei Wei clinging to a rock. He had shed his pack and escorted her back to the top and a significant distance down the other side. When Dad showed up and agreed to accompany her down the rest of the way, the Finnish hiker turned around and headed up over the Death Pass for the third time that afternoon.

Angela & Wei Wei

Wei Wei had a reservation at a hotel in Griesalp, and since we were heading in that direction (and she was obviously completely panic-stricken from what she'd just experienced), we walked together for the next 2 hours as the piles of rocks which showed the way down the otherwise unmarked precipitous slope turned into an actual footpath which eventually turned into a gravel road.

Wei Wei was very insistent on following the road-signs for Griesalp. Often on these climbs and descents, a trail will cut down a hill or through the woods as the road takes a long switchback around. In those situations we take the trails, both to save walking time and to spare our feet from walking on the hard roads. Having done this for 2 weeks, we recognized the shortcuts immediately, but Wei Wei was not convinced. We spent several minutes assuring her that either way we'd end up in the same place. We even pointed it out to her on her map – "This is where we are. This is the trail right here. You're following this red line, which goes aaaaaaaalll the way around here before ending up in the exact same spot." But she insisted on following her red line. Meanwhile we, sick of walking and looking for an isolated place to camp, parted ways with her.

It was maybe 10 or 15 minutes before our shortcut met back with the road, and then we were 5 minutes down the next shortcut when we saw Wei Wei on the road high above us. We waved. I almost climbed back up, just to say, "See, I told you so," but that wouldn't have been very gentlemanly, and besides it would've meant an extra 10 minutes of walking.

We found a fabulous place to camp at a Feuerstelle right next to the river. It was fairly well exposed, which always results in the paranoia that we might get arrested in the middle of the night. But we'd been walking for 10 hours and it was a flat spot to pitch our tents. For that we were always willing to risk spending the night in jail.

For dinner we had the following options:
- Instant noodles
- Instant soup with crackers
- Crackers and tuna fish
- Instant mashed potatoes and tuna fish

- Instant mashed potatoes with dried sausage
- Instant soup with peanut butter and jelly
- Instant soup with dried sausage and tuna fish

Naturally, these were the same options we'd had every single other time we'd camped out away from a town, and although these foods all happen to be highly rich in the nutrients one needs when hiking for 7 hours a day, you can only have so many meals of mashed potatoes and tuna fish in a 2-week period before you start to get sick of it. I'm sure we did eat that night, but my brain has repressed the memory.

The following morning Angela and I were awake before Dad. Shock! Horror! Several times a family or a large group of school kids would walk noisily past Dad's tent, and still he didn't move. We began to get scared, and when he was still asleep at 8:30 I checked to make sure he was still breathing. In the meantime, as the sun hadn't yet risen over the mountains, it was ridiculously cold. Angela and I made hot apple cider, but it only warmed up our stomachs and not our outer layers of skin, which was the part that was cold to begin with.

The mountain to our east cast its shadow over the mountain to the west, and we spent half an hour watching the shadow line move down toward us as the sun rose up. It reminded me of the scene in *The Mummy Returns* when they're running to make it into the golden pyramid before the sun comes up.[10]

Somewhere along the way we'd heard that this day's hike – to Kandersteg – was supposed to be even tougher than the one we'd gone over the day before. I can hear the announcer now:

"Angela vs. Death Pass II. The last time these two met, they fought for twelve rounds, and in the end, Angela won it on a split decision. What do you think of that decision, Max?"

"Well, it's obvious that Angela fought that bout scared, and

---

[10] Did I actually just confess to having seen and **remembered** *The Mummy Returns*? Never mind, forget I said anything.

Death Pass certainly put her to the test, but in the end he just didn't have what it took to put the bout away. But this time, Death Pass is back with a vengeance. He's been training hard, he's put on 550 feet, he's got more ice in his step, he's got a steeper uppercut. I don't think she can take him. My prediction: the ref calls it for Death Pass in the 11th round."

There happened to be a map of the area right next to the Feuerstelle, and while Dad packed up, Angela and I studied it and identified an alternative route – north down the valley to Kiental, and then veer east into Interlaken, from where we knew we'd be able to get to Zurich easily. Just at that moment, who should walk by? Wei Wei, on her way to the Second Death Pass of Doom. We had suggested to her the day before that often it's possible to find a valley route around, and here we had found one for certain. Well before Kiental, she'd be able to break off west again and go over a much easier pass before dropping back into the Kandersteg valley. We estimated the whole thing would take about the same length of time, but her chances of falling off a cliff somewhere would be far more remote.

But as before, she was very insistent on sticking to her map. While we were arguing with her, the group of Swiss hikers that we'd encountered several times the day before came up. They, too, had spent the night in Griesalp. We explained to them the situation and they agreed to shepherd Wei Wei up and over Death Pass II to Kandersteg.

After bidding them goodbye, Dad, Angela and I broke camp and started down the valley. About 3 minutes into our walk we came upon a sign that posted the regulations for the local municipality. There were illustrations of a dog on a leash, a person picking up after a dog defecating on the ground, and a picture of a tent with a big red line through it. We didn't have a dog, but it was pretty clear that the last illustration meant that we had camped illegally the previous night. We figured if we ever got caught we could just plead ignorance – "We're sorry, we don't understand German illustrations." Fortunately we didn't get caught, though now that I've confessed my crime in writing, we will never again be able to return to Switzerland for fear of being immediately arrested at immigration control.

But no matter. It was a beautiful, sunny day, the first we'd had in 2 weeks that was completely rain-free. Onward we hastened, and after only 2 hours we came to Kiental, a beautiful, isolated valley town. According to the various people and maps we consulted, the local private campsite would be the last for another 12-15 miles, so we made the conservative call and decided to spend the night there.

It was only lunchtime, but you'd be amazed how easily you can kill an entire day when life has slowed down to a mountaineer's pace. We spent 90 minutes perched on the front steps of the grocery store, waiting for it to open so we could eat something other than peanut butter and jelly crackers for lunch. We walked down the hill to the campsite, set up our tents, and washed our clothes. Angela and I walked back up the hill to the grocery store and spent 45 minutes agonizing over what to buy for dinner. We then spent half an hour preparing our salad, ate it slowly, chatted for a little while, and then spent 45 minutes preparing dinner. We ate, washed the dishes, and then spent 3 hours watching the clouds. As we sat there on a bench, a string of tiny cumulus clouds raced across an otherwise clear sky squeezing between the Blumlisalp, (the tallest mountain in the area) and a shorter peak just in front of it, and coming out the other side as a much denser mass. As a result, it was 2½ hours before we caught a view of the Blumlisalp that was completely unobscured, and when we did we were almost disappointed that the constant eclipse had finally been broken.

Eventually the sun went down and the temperature dropped, forcing us into the shelter of our tents for the night.

The Cast in Kiental

We Love to Go A-wandering Along the Mountain Weg

Don   **July 7th- 9th**

When I got up for my middle of the night micturation, there were stars by the millions. What a relief to anticipate another clear day. Yeah, right!

It looked as though the first portion of the walk would be on road, so we decided to take the bus the first 5 miles from Kiental to Reichenbach. From there we headed east on the Panoramaweg along the heights above the Thünersee, one of the two lakes that abut Interlaken. The path was extremely varied – up, down, farm, forest, canyons, rivers and stupendous views. After about 3 hours of sun, though, the sky suddenly clouded over and we walked the next 4 hours to Interlaken in rain: light rain, torrential rain, drizzle, misty rain, driving rain, and a few types of rain for which there is probably no term yet. Even so, it was a beautiful walk.

Since this was our last day's walk with Angela, it seems like a good time to tell you a bit more about how we would amuse ourselves during the long hours on the trail. Sometimes, when the terrain was suitable – road or wide trails without much slope – we'd walk next to each other. At those times we'd often sing songs, usually substituting comical, relevant lyrics for the original words. For example, "Away out here they got a name for rain and rain and rain. The rain is Tess, the rain is Tess, and they call the rain … Tess." Or, "I love to go a-wandering along the mountain weg. And as I go, I love to drink, from any nearby keg." Or, when we passed by the village of Schattdorff, "Schatt through the heartdorff, and you're to blame … ." What did you expect from extemporaneous lyrics, Oscar Hammerstein?

Another way we would occupy our time was to play a punning game that I invented about 15 years earlier when Rhonda and I were visiting Tintern Abbey in Wales. The word "tintinnabulation" is a 50 cent word referring to the sound of ringing bells. As we were walking around the abbey, I asked Rhonda, "What did they call it when the nuns walked around when the bells were ringing? Tinternambulation. And what do you call the feeling of joy that the nuns got when they were walking around and the bells started ringing? Tintern Abbey elation. The nuns dancing when the bells were ringing? Tinternundulation. The nuns anointing themselves in the fountain while the bells were ringing? Tintern Abbey ablution." You get the idea. David grew up with the game, and now we taught it to Angela. So when any of us would use a multi-syllable word, it would generate some period of "Tintern Abbey" style puns. Imagine, for example, that I used the word "confrontation" in a sentence. David would say, "What would you call it if somebody threatened you with a container of peas? It would be a "can-frontation."

And Angela would say, "And if a bunch of people escaped from prison and went to grow bananas in Central America?" We'd try to figure it out, but usually couldn't, and she'd chime in with delight, "A con-plantation."

This would go on anywhere from a few minutes to an hour or more until a word would run down. ("Tintern Abbey" lasted me on and off for years.) Then, we'd talk about something else for a while until someone would use another multi-syllable word, and away we'd go again.

It was still pouring when we walked the last few miles on paths next to or on the hillside just above the busy road into Interlaken. We found Interlaken to be a frantically touristy place. There were dozens of restaurants and tourist shops filled with people of every color. The menus and other signs on the streets were in a wide range of languages; surprisingly, the most prevalent after English was Korean. I suppose Interlaken is okay for visitors who don't know any better, but after experiencing dozens of idyllic, non-touristy towns and villages over the previous weeks, David and I agreed that we would be glad to be back on the trail and away from civilization again.

For dinner we found our way to a Chinese/Thai restaurant – our first non-Swiss or camp stove meal in 3 weeks. It was a surreal experience communicating with a Chinese waiter in German. You just don't expect to hear someone speaking German with a Chinese accent. We also got the impression that we might have stumbled on an organized crime front – when we arrived there was a 20-year-old Chinese kid dressed to the nines, with his jacket hung over his shoulders like a Mafia don. He looked to be very much in charge. At one point the middle-aged waiter told him something, and though we couldn't understand what they were saying, their body language implied we might have been about to see someone get whacked.

Fortunately, the food was outstanding. What is it about crime front restaurants that the food is so good? When I worked at the Opel[11] manufacturing plant in Rüsselsheim, Germany, I used to frequent a Greek restaurant located above a warehouse. It was a large place with about 30 tables, inexpensively priced, and with fantastic food. I averaged eating there about once a week for the 12 years from 1985 to 1996. But in all that time, I only ever saw one other customer. I kept asking myself, how can they afford to stay in business? Then one day when I was going past the warehouse entrance downstairs, I thought to look at the signs. The building also housed the offices of the local longshoreman's union. Aha, I thought. This restaurant doesn't have to make money. Just launder it.

We'd originally been planning on spending the night in a campground, of which there were eight or 10 in the city, but the pouring rain when we got there convinced us to try to find a hotel. We asked the restaurant owner for a recommendation for a quiet, cheap hotel and he steered us to a one-star place a block away which

---

[11] Opel is a European automobile manufacturer owned by General Motors. I spent 15 years off and on working with them while I lived in Europe. Every time I even think about my time working with GM I have trouble convincing myself not to jump off a bridge. But that's another story.

had one 3-bedded room left. After the mandatory showers, clothes washing in the sink and stringing of clotheslines across the room, we settled into our bunks. Before we nodded off to sleep, David informed me that he was fed up with the constant rain. What about trying somewhere else in Europe where it might be drier? Since David's into wine and speaks French, he suggested the Rhône Valley in France. I countered with the fact that the Rhône Valley is awfully flat for hiking. What about the southeast portion of France above Monaco, or Tuscany in Italy? We might still get rain in those places, though, so I suggested the Canary Islands, where it rains about once a year. We agreed we'd talk about it more on the way to Zurich the next day.

It poured all that night, but it didn't bother us so much because we had a roof over our heads. Gotcha, rain gods! In the morning I got onto the Internet and reserved a car to drive to Zurich to drop off Angela. We tried the same website that got us "such a good deal" in London, and had considerably more luck this time. There was an Avis agency about 2 blocks from the hotel, and when I arrived (no more than 5 minutes after making the reservation) the clerk told me that the price I'd gotten was much better than if I'd just walked in and asked for a car. Let that be a lesson to everyone.

We drove to Zurich, about 2 hours in heavy traffic and heavier rain. We even got a military escort – dozens of tanks and armored personnel carriers seemed to be making the same journey we were. Half way to Zurich, a car in front of us kicked up a stone and cracked the windshield. Not a chip; a crack halfway across from the left to the middle. On the instructions of my credit card company I had declined the extra insurance; there would be no trouble with them paying if there was damage to the car, they assured me. As I sit writing this in Colorado 4 months after our return, I'm still fighting with Visa over their commitment to cover the extortionate repair costs – $900 to replace a windshield. Maybe it wasn't such a good idea to have taunted the rain gods. Let that be a lesson to everyone, too.

High Society

David July 9th

When we arrived at Elena and Tomas's house in Zurich, they were absolutely beside themselves, having worried the whole time that we might have fallen off a mountain somewhere. Angela went down to the basement immediately to change into a set of clean clothes, and when she returned she was positively beaming because the jeans that had been tight 2 weeks ago were now about half a size too big.

We had another fabulous lunch and shared our experiences from the past 3 weeks – the towns we'd been to, the skilifts we'd slept in, and so on. Every time we mentioned the name of a town or a pass, no matter how small, Tomas would smile and nod with recognition, saying something like, "Aah, yes, Kiental. Aah." I couldn't help but think he resembled Albert Einstein. Or that guy from the movie *Wolf* who tells Jack Nicholson, "That's very auspicious!"

One of the things Dad didn't mention about Elena is that, as my surrogate grandmother, when I was a child I liked her a whole lot better than I liked him and Mom. I used to ride my skateboard the several blocks to her house, stand out front and shout up through the open window, "Elena, can I come in?!" particularly when my parents had done something that upset me, like making me clean my room. For a while they were a little afraid that they'd come home one evening to find I'd gone away with Elena, never to return. But the one time I packed a suitcase and ran away to her house she promptly returned me home (much to my dismay). I think that alleviated their fears somewhat.

As a linguist, Elena had helped teach me German, and being an amateur photographer she took photographs of me all the time. There was one in particular that featured me with my shirt off, sporting my 8-year-old puppy fat, and holding a yellow rose in full bloom. That photo, needless to say, made its way out to show off to Angela, and after dinner we all sat on the couch for Elena to take pictures – first of the three of us, then of me with Angela, and finally of just me, because "You're just so handsome."

As Dad and I re-packed our bags, shuffled items, refilled our Campsuds, and absorbed some of the supplies Angela was carrying, Elena packed several pieces of the chocolate cake she'd made for dessert. It weighed about 6 lbs, but it was so outstanding we took it with us anyway and ate it for the next week until it started to turn fuzzy and change colors. I also had to store my walking stick in the basement for the next 6 weeks, since I would be assuming Angela's trekking poles. It was a teary goodbye. In Lauterbrunnen I'd drawn a face on the stick and knighted it with the prestigious name and title Sir Wilson Lütschintal the Umlaut – Wilson after the volleyball in *Cast Away*, Lütschintal because it was the coolest sounding name of all the towns we'd been through thus far, and Umlaut because it's a diacritic that replaces the tittle when the lowercase vowel is an *i*, and was historically preceded by the trema which dates back to the Byzantine Empire.[12]

Sir Wilson Lütschintal the Umlaut

---

[12] Actually, I just thought it was funny. But now you can show off to all your friends how much you know about umlauts.

I'd grown very attached to Sir Wilson and on the road to Kiental I'd made Angela kiss him for good weatherluck. It had worked (for 24 hours, at least), so before storing him in the basement for the next 6 weeks, I made Angela kiss him another 45 times, once for each day left to go.

As we were on our way out, Elena expressed her approval of Angela and then offered her some of the most horrendous relationship advice I'd ever heard in my life. Things like "Never shed a tear for a man," and "Always keep him at a distance, wondering." Angela smiled and nodded, but so far has been smart enough to continue acting as though she actually likes me.

We spent the rest of the day touring Zurich. The city has 4 old churches within a few blocks of each other – Fraumünster,

Grossmünster, St. Peter's Church, and Eglise Française, which translate to Lady Cathedral, Big Cathedral, St. Peter's Church, and, of course, French Church. You'd think the Swiss would realize that they can't fool people into thinking their places of worship have clever names simply by using a language other than English.

But what their churches lacked in sobriquetic creativity, they more than made up for in their magnificence and atmosphere. In the first church we visited, a pianist and a string quartet were doing the sound check for a concert they were going to perform that evening. It was amazing! (Of course churches tend to have magnificent acoustics even when they're not a thousand years old and constructed out of marble.)

In the Grossmünster, we paid a couple of francs per person to walk up the steps – first stone, then oak, then cedar, and then pine – the materials used in construction getting less durable as the church was expanded over the centuries – to the top of the spire, which was the highest point in Zurich. It's not quite the same as the rotating restaurants at the top of San Antonio's Tower of Americas or Las Vegas' Stratosphere, but staring out at the miles of houses that make up Zurich's suburbs was certainly a different view than we'd been used to for the past couple of weeks.

Most impressive of all, though, were the Chagall Windows at Fraumünster – a series of tall stained glass windows created by Marc Chagall depicting various images of Christianity. Dad and I marveled at the courage it takes to hire a Jewish Russian-American cubist to design the stained glass windows for the renovation of a 9th century Swiss church.

As we headed toward the final church, we heard an orchestra performing a classical piece. But when we turned the corner toward the courtyard we discovered it wasn't an orchestra at all but a single man playing the accordion. We stood and watched in awe as this one man filled up the entire courtyard with his music.

We walked down Bahnhofstrasse, which is known for its designer boutiques, designer jewelry stores, and designer banks. We passed stores with names like Cartier, Bulgari, and Philippe Patek, displaying trenchcoats that cost $8,000 and necklaces that cost

$200,000. The lobbies of the private banks consisted of little more than a few pieces of fine art and a receptionist with more equity in her breasts than most people have in their homes.

Of course, the Swiss banking tradition is a notorious one – once upon a time, Swiss banks offered no interest and charged an annual fee for the privilege of having them hold your money. They knew exactly why their foreign customers were choosing a Swiss bank to store enormous sums of cash, and the greater the annual fee, the fewer questions they asked. Nowadays, that's less common, particularly among the "Big Five" banks. Nonetheless, under Swiss law tax evasion is a political offense, not a criminal one, which attracts a lot of business from people seeking to avoid inheritance taxes and government involvement in divorce, bankruptcy, and other personal wealth disputes. On the other hand, the Swiss government charges a 35% tax on interest, most of which foreigners can get back, but only by proving they aren't Swiss residents, which opens the account up to public scrutiny and negates most of the reasons for storing your money in Switzerland to begin with.

With dinner fast approaching and our pockets getting poorer with every second our car remained in the downtown parking garage (more on that in the next chapter), we began to head back. Reaching the car, Dad suddenly had a revelation and started jumping up and down with excitement. "I know where we'll go for dinner!" he exclaimed. "Mamma Mia's!" Mamma Mia's is an Italian restaurant near where he used to work, and Dad's all time favorite restaurant in Switzerland. He used to go there at least once a week, and he'd always get the calzone. The one time he didn't, he regretted it, and for the last 15 years we've all had to put up with him lamenting that, "In the last moment before the truck runs me down, when my life flashes before my eyes, my one regret is going to be that I once ate in Mamma Mia's and didn't get the calzone."

While we certainly appreciated Dad's desire to eat at his favorite restaurant, Angela and I weren't especially excited about the idea of eating at an Italian restaurant on our only night in Zurich. We'd already discussed the idea of trying to ditch Dad for a night alone, so this provided the perfect excuse. "Why don't you go to Mamma

Mia's and we'll fend for ourselves," we suggested, to which he readily agreed.

We did just that, checking into the hotel and then walking back down Bahnhofstrasse to the Zeughauskeller Gildhalle, an old armory that's been converted into a restaurant. The menus are in about a dozen languages and feature 30 different kinds of sausage, and in order to meet demand they'll sit multiple parties together at the same table, which put us at the end of a rectangular 6-top.

It was not exactly the height of romance, eating beer and brats and rubbing elbows with a pair of Swiss businessmen, but the food was outstanding, even if they were a little stingy with the portions. Afterwards we seriously considered going for a second meal of döner kebab (the Pakistani equivalent of a gyro, and the ethnic fast food of choice throughout much of Europe), but resisted the temptation. Instead, we returned to our hotel to rearrange the furniture – because the room was long and skinny, the twin beds were placed head-to-head, which was not exactly what we had in mind when we asked for a room for two. Fortunately the room was wide enough to place the beds next to each other, provided we didn't want to open the closet or use the desk.

This also put our beds directly in front of the window. Now, in an effort to keep this book PG-13 I have, until this point, avoided going into detail on how adventurous two twenty-somethings can get, even when their chaperone is sleeping (or perhaps not sleeping) 6 feet away. There was, for example, the "nap" that Angela and I took in Lauterbrunnen while Dad was reading the *Herald Trib*. There was also the campsite in Elm when a huge thunderstorm passed over; when Dad headed to our tent to grab a cooking pot the following morning I had to stop him because I wasn't sure where we'd left the conjugal evidence. And there was the night in the skilift, which I didn't relay 100% accurately.

On this particular night we had no such concerns, but, as I said, we did have our bed right in front of the window. So again, in an effort to keep this book PG-13, let's just say that it wouldn't surprise me if there's now a picture of us floating on the Internet that was taken with someone's cell phone.

Racing up the Mountain

Don   **July 10th**

Our accommodations were at the Martahof Hotel, which we'd found listed in a Swiss backpacker's magazine in our hotel room in Interlaken. A typical basic room in Zurich starts at 120 francs per person (~$100) and goes up to 1,000 francs. If you are willing to put up with really lousy service and the toilet and shower being down the hall, you can go as low as 50 francs person. And if you're willing to sleep in a room with six strangers and bring your own sheets, you can find something for 32 francs. Since this was David and Angela's last night together and they had spent a lot of nights either in the same room as me or in sleeping bags in tents 10 feet away from me, I decided to treat them to a double room, which was only 98 francs for the two of them. I was in a six-bedded dorm room – but each person had a curtained off 6-foot x 7-foot area – for 40 francs.

The Martahof is in the center of Zurich, right across the river from the train station, and conveniently located within 100 yards of 10 sex shops, 4 strip clubs, and 3 porno movie theaters. Sure, it's a little noisy, but at least parking is cheap – about $80 a day in the nearby parking garage and $30 a day in meters on the street. That is if: a) you feel like moving your car every 2 hours all day long, and; b) you can find places by meters, which you can't. I remember when Rhonda and I were touring Europe in 1974, we ended up driving around Zurich for 2 hours and then abandoning the city because we couldn't find a place to park that we could afford. It's nice to know that nothing has changed in 33 years.

With all the sex-related action going on in the area, it turned out that the street outside my window was the congregating point for a group of rowdy night-life participants who talked loudly and gunned their motorcycle engines until after midnight. Then the skies opened up again and they all scattered. I certainly never expected to be so delighted to see it pouring rain again so soon.

Nonetheless, the forecast for later that week was actually for improving weather, so David and I resolved to at least finish the trek across Switzerland before taking off for sunnier climes.

We dropped Angela off at the Zurich airport and drove to Interlaken where we returned the car. The man at the Avis desk was very nice and tried to insist that he'd drive us to the train station, which was all of 3 blocks away. Instead, we walked to the hotel we'd stayed in 2 nights before for David to use their Internet terminal to check his e-mail. The hotel clerk was a heavily tattooed young man with pieces of metal looped through every visible square inch of skin (and, no doubt, in many less visible places). He said he would be happy to let us use the terminal, but one of his previous customers had reset the operating system from the German to the U.S. keyboard layout, so he couldn't get anything to work. David and I have the U.S. keyboard memorized, but that wasn't much consolation for him, so we switched it back, and he was so delighted that he let David use the terminal for free.

We went to the local Migros to stock up on groceries and then stopped at a hole-in-the-wall döner kebab restaurant for a last junk meal before heading to the station to catch the train back to Reichenbach. If you've never taken public transportation in Switzerland, you're missing a real treat. With your ticket they give you a detailed itinerary explaining every move you have to make, down to the second. Train A leaves from Track B at Time C. It arrives in Town D at Track E at Time F. Your connecting train leaves from Track G 2 minutes later. You arrive at Town H at Time I. Then you walk around the corner where Bus J will leave 3 minutes later. Bus J will arrive on top of mountain K in the middle of nowhere 27 minutes later. And you can set your watch on it every step of the way. It's a hell of a shock after living in the UK for 20 years. In the UK you're lucky if the train you're taking leaves on the day it's scheduled to leave; when it's going to arrive is anybody's guess. There was a period of time when I was commuting into

London and counted 40 days in a row that I wasn't able to get from station to station unimpeded by trains arriving late, trains breaking down, escalators under construction, entrances closed, and even the occasional train leaving early, which meant I'd miss my scheduled train and have to wait up to an hour for the next one.

We arrived in Reichenbach exactly when we were scheduled to. And I mean to the second. We walked out of the train station – surprise! – into a rain shower. I knew the weather was just baiting me, so I refused to put my rain gear on for 5 minutes while the rain got harder and harder. Finally, I capitulated and put it on; within 30 seconds the rain stopped and the sun came out. I took the rain gear back off and within 2 minutes it got overcast and started to drizzle. But I'd learned my lesson, so I walked for the next 5 hours in varying degrees of rain and fog, getting wetter and wetter, but without donning the rain gear again.

One of the last pieces of advice that Angela gave David before she left was to dispense with Wilson Lütschintal and use the trekking poles so he could "smoke" me. I told David that it would be a while yet before he could manage that. As we walked up the first steep hills out of Reichenbach, we started going faster and faster, each trying not to show the other how desperate we were – him to leave me behind, and me not to be left behind – by breaking into a run. For 45 minutes we sparred back and forth, sometimes with David a few feet ahead and sometimes with me ahead, and completely exhausted ourselves. Eventually, we reached a truce and proceeded at a more reasonable pace.

At 6:05 pm we walked into Adelboden and found a cute little campground. On the door was a sign saying that the office closed at 6:00 pm and instructing us to call a certain number if we arrived after hours. I pulled out the cell-phone we'd purchased in Altdorf and, as had become customary any time we needed to use it, spent the next 5 minutes cursing profusely at the damn thing because I could never figure out how to unlock the keypad. Just as I was getting ready to throw the phone into the street, David tried the office door. It was open, and the proprietor was sitting at the desk inside. I wish I'd thought of that!

We checked in and bought a couple of beers and a bag of paprika potato chips to supplement what we'd been carrying in our backpacks. The proprietor showed us a room with a table and chairs where we could cook and eat out of the rain. By the time we finished pitching our tents and carried our food and stove into the room, two women had salad fixings spread out on the table and were preparing a meal. I heard them speaking a Slavic language and said a few words to them in Russian. They gave me a dirty look – it turns out they were from Prague. When am I going to learn that Czechs and Poles would prefer not to be addressed in Russian? No lasting harm was done, though. One of the women had lived 4 years in New York and spoke reasonable English. We had quite a nice conversation while we cooked and ate.

By this time, I had gotten good enough at setting up my tent that I was reasonably confident of staying dry on rainy nights. Until I had to pee, that is. I hated so much having to get out of my warm, cozy sleeping bag, sometimes several times a night, that for several weeks I had been working on what I dubbed "P4" – the Partially Prone Peeing Position. I'd keep my feet in the sleeping bag inside the tent, extend my torso into the rain with my hands on the ground and my arms extended in a push-up position, pull out Peter, and try not to pee on my hands.

It was that night in Adelboden that I perfected it. (It's only now that I have confirmation of my application for registration of P4 with the U.S. Patent Office that I can reveal the details of how it works.) On the next page is a copy of a portion of that night's letter, including a drawing of P4. I guess now it should be called P5 – the Patented Partially Prone Peeing Position.

2-19

AND EAT. BY THE TIME WE'D PITCHED
OUR TENTS, 2 WOMEN FROM THE
CZECH REPUBLIC WERE ALSO IN
THE ROOM. ONE OF THEM HAD
LIVED FOR 4 YEARS IN NEW YORK
& SPOKE REASONABLE ENGLISH.
WE HAD QUITE A NICE
CONVERSATION WHILE WE COOKED
AND ATE.

NOW I AM IN MY TENT AND IT'S
STARTING TO RAIN PRETTY HARD,
BUT I SHOULD BE DRY & COZY
FOR THE NIGHT. UNTIL I
HAVE TO PEE, ANYWAY. THEN
IT WILL BE TIME FOR MY NEWLY
PATENTED P4 - PARTIALLY
PRONE PEEING POSITION - IN
WHICH I KEEP MY FEET INSIDE
THE TENT, EXTEND MY TORSO
OUT INTO THE RAIN WITH MY
ARMS HANDS ON THE GROUND AND

2-20

MY ARMS EXTENDED IN A PUSH-UP
POSITION, AND TRY NOT TO
PEE ON MY HANDS.

WELL, THAT'S IT FOR TONIGHT.
IT'S POURING NOW & TIME
FOR ME TO BATTEN DOWN THE
HATCHES.
TOMORROW IS A 4½ HOUR
WALK TO LENK.
LOVE + REGARDS, Don

---

11 JULY 2007
LENK

DEAR FAMILY + FRIENDS,
IT'S BEEN A VERY EVENTFUL DAY TODAY-
AT LEAST AS FAR AS WALKING BETWEEN
SMALL TOWNS IN THE ALPS CAN BE
EVENTFUL. WE CLIMBED OUT OF
THE SKI RESORT OF ADELBODEN AT 9:20
THIS MORNING. THE WALK TO LENK
WAS SUPPOSED TO TAKE US 4½ HOURS.
UNFORTUNATELY, WE FOLLOWED A SIGN
TO HANNEMOOSPASS, OUR INTERMEDIATE
POINT, WHICH, INSTEAD OF TAKING
US BY THE SHORTEST + EASIEST ROUTE,
TOOK US ON A ROUGH UPHILL
CLIMB ONTO AN EXPOSED RIDGE
BEFORE ABANDONING US IN THE
SNOW ABOVE 2000 METERS. BY
THE TIME WE FOUND A WAY DOWN
TO A TRAIL THAT EVENTUALLY
TOOK US TO HANNEMOOSPASS, WE
HAD BEEN WALKING FOR 4 HOURS
ON A PORTION OF THE ROUTE THAT

2

WAS SUPPOSED TO TAKE US 2
HOURS, AND WE WERE TIRED +
COLD & WET. DID I MENTION THAT
IT WAS RAINING ALL DAY? A
FROM HANNEMOOS PASS WE BEAT
A HASTY RETREAT DOWN THE
HILL TO WARMER WEATHER. BY
THE WAY, HANNEMOOSPASS IS
FAMOUS FOR MODEL AIRPLANE
FLYING & SOMETHING ABOUT THE
CONSTANT UPHILL WINDS. DAVID
+ I WALKED INTO A BUILDING
THAT SAID IT WAS A RESTAURANT
INSTEAD IT WAS PACKED WITH
PEOPLE MAKING ADJUSTMENTS
+ REPAIRS + PREPARATIONS TO
HUNDREDS OR MODEL PLANES.
WE SAW SEVERAL PLANES FLYING AS
WELL, BUT MOST OF THE
PEOPLE SEEMED TO BE
WAITING FOR BETTER WEATHER.

Showing Off Leads to Exhaustion

David   **July 11th-12th**

In the morning, I got up early and sat in the breakfast room to write. The entire trip Dad seemed to thrive on writing massive quantities every single evening and then mailing it back home to 50 people who couldn't possibly have cared to read that much. I've always felt especially lazy after a tough workout and a big meal, and writing takes an awful lot of mental energy, so getting into the tent at night, the last thing I had the energy for was writing. When you add in the fact that campsites often had breakfast rooms that were a comparatively humane temperature while our tents often fell somewhere in the 40° F range, I much preferred doing my writing in the morning.

Dad joined me after a while, and we ate the muesli we'd come to expect for breakfast. I'd gotten a new kind for that day – more complex carbs, less fat, less sugar, and far, far less taste. We also ate some peaches Dad had been carrying for the last 3 days. By now he would no longer allow me to carry any food that was bruisable, crushable, smooshable, or otherwise even remotely destructible, since it was guaranteed to end up in its highest state of entropy within minutes. Before the ban we constantly found ourselves washing off food packets that were covered in butter, jam, or chocolate that had once been in a sealed container but had long since exploded inside my backpack. Meanwhile, Dad could carry around peaches, potato chips, and bananas, and 3 days later they'd still be in perfect condition. I'm not sure how he managed it, but it provided a great excuse for me to make him carry most of the food.

The road to Lenk was supposed to be fairly easy and gradual the whole way. Unfortunately the trail signs turned on us at a rather crucial point. We reached a junction where the sign pointed in one direction to Hahnenmoos and the other direction to Hahnenmoospass. Since we knew we were supposed to go the Hahnenmoospass, that's the sign we followed, figuring that Hahnenmoos was the town below or near the pass, and not where we wanted to go.

The trail in this direction was much tougher than we were anticipating, featuring a number of switchbacks, avalanche breakers, and a trail of (wet) vegetation at roughly calf height that soaked through our pants. We were expecting to hit the pass in an hour, but after an hour and a half we reached another junction with a trail marker indicating it was another 1 hour and 15 minutes to the Hahnenmoospass. Off in the distance we spotted a few buildings at the top of a pass and wondered if that was it. "But surely," we thought, "if that was it, they would have just directed us straight up that gently sloping valley rather than here on the Bergweg of Despair and then along the Pointy Ridge of Danger. We were confused and more than a little pissed off.

For the next hour, we walked along the aforementioned Ridge of Danger on the aforementioned Bergweg of Despair, ultimately reaching a massive plateau with no signs. We stood there in ankle-deep snow deciding which direction to head for just long enough to allow the ice to penetrate our shoes and freeze our toes.

As it turned out, the buildings we had seen in the distance were, in fact, the Hahnenmoospass, and when we got there we discovered there was no difference between that and Hahnenmoos – they just put the two names on the sign pointing in different directions to throw off tourists and amuse the locals. A sign at Hahnenmoos pointed back toward Adelboden 2 hours the normal way, and about 4 hours the way we had come. We felt thoroughly shafted, and all I could say to Dad was, "Boy am I glad Angela wasn't here to blame you for this."

Hahnenmoospass, apparently, is famous for its model glider airplane flying, which is to say the winds are consistently of a force that would make a fire-hydrant turn its back and run. Between the altitude, the wind, the rain, and not having seen the sun in 4 days, it was, to use the charming Southern expression, colder than a witch's tit. We walked into the cafeteria, which was serving no food as it was overrun by people making adjustments and repairs and preparations to hundreds of model airplanes. So we found a secluded exterior corner of a building that was slightly sheltered from the wind, ate our peanut butter and cracker lunch, and then crouched in the bathroom under the automatic hand dryer for half an hour to try to get the feeling back in our fingers and toes

We got to Lenk at around 4 in the afternoon. The campground building was being renovated and scaffolding decorated the exterior, but the owner greeted us straight away and told us to make ourselves at home. We did so, during the only hour of sun we had that day, and then washed our clothes in a tub *with a washboard in it.* Did you hear that? The tub had a washboard! We were so excited we could hardly contain ourselves.

Perhaps because of our trek story and perhaps because we were the only customers there, the owner and his wife promptly adopted us. They presented us with a 2-pound hunk of Alpkäse that had to be worth more than the CHF 22 we were paying to pitch our tents. And because of the rain, they even offered to let us stay for no charge in one of the caravans they usually rent out. We were shocked and moved, but assured them that we were used to camping in the rain and couldn't put them through the trouble of having to service the caravan after we left. In the morning, they led us into their private kitchen so we didn't have to eat our breakfast outside in the cold. We wondered if they'd just bought the place – that would certainly explain the renovations and all they were going through to make us happy, but they said they'd owned it for years (I can't remember exactly how many). The lack of other clientele was just because it was still early in the season that high, and it was even less busy than normal because of the rain.

At the end of the Lenk valley was a massive cliff. I'd spent part of the evening before watching the rain clouds blow up the valley, reach the cliff and then just stop, hover, and drop rain endlessly over the same spot. The rain did pass over during the course of the night, and the next day dawned cold, clear and bright.

Although we had thought about taking a rest day, Dad and I both wanted to spend a day walking in the sun, so we headed on to Lauenen. The trip to Lauenen was supposed to be a tough one. The climb was 3,000 feet, and though it was fairly gradual, the mud was nasty for the second half of that. At some point I noticed that I was maybe 20 yards in front of Dad, and realized that this was my opportunity to take off.

Some background on "smoking Dad." We've already mentioned Dad's habit of leaving his walking partners far behind without a second thought. He says that "his mind takes over" and he "gets into the rhythm of walking," and refers to Bill Bryson's *A Walk in the Woods* to corroborate that excuse, since Bryson mentions a similar experience in that book. Personally, I think it's a rather feeble excuse – not that there's any conscious or malicious intent behind it, but we'd spent the last 3 weeks on the exact same hike, and I never once got more than about 5 yards in front of Angela. Of course, on those rare occasions when Mom and Dad go for a walk together, he does a much better job of keeping a reasonable pace, because she's very good at reminding him not to walk too far ahead. She'll say subtle things like, "I'm really sick of looking at your ass, Don," to which Dad usually replies, "But a fine ass it is." Angela was also pretty good at sending me subtle reminders, but I realize I'm bordering dangerously close to comparing my fiancée to her future mother-in-law, so I'll stop here, before I put my foot in mouth any further.

Anyway, after Dad and my grandfather did the long walk from Lands End to John O' Groats, the family often heard stories of Dad repeatedly leaving Grandpa "in the dust," particularly when they were going uphill. It was always said as a joke, but you could tell that Grandpa was just a little bitter about it, and he wasn't altogether laughing on the inside. So when we were getting ready to leave for our trip to Europe, Grandpa took me aside and said, "Promise me something, David. Promise me that you will leave him in the dust. *In the dust.*" I promised him I would. Angela didn't make me promise anything, but she did make it clear that she would appreciate me avenging her as well.

This was how Dad and I found ourselves racing up the hill from the Reichenbach train station. And here, as I found myself 20 yards in front of him, knowing that he hates walking in mud and that he'd take detours and cautious steps the whole time, I plowed through, moving as fast as I could to try to leave him and make good on my promise to grandpa and Angela.

At one point, I looked back and was surprised I didn't see him. "I must be further ahead than I thought," I said to myself. I plowed on. I was quite out of breath and my legs were achy, but I had to put more distance between us.

Eventually I reached a point where I wasn't sure I'd made the right choice of route, so I stopped and waited for him to show up. After about 5 minutes he appeared in the distance, so I took a picture (for evidence) and waited another 5 or 10 minutes for him to catch up to me. I don't know that it quite constituted leaving him in the dust, but it's about as well as I could've done, given that Dad could keep up with me in just about every other situation. *(Note from Don: I object! I walked in rain and mud for thousands of miles in England and I know how miserable it can be if you get water in your shoes. So I make sure not to do it. David is completely oblivious and just plows ahead. Next time, I demand that he lets me know if we are racing. Bastard!) (Response from David: As you can tell, Dad's still a little sensitive about this one.) (Interjection from Angela: Take that, footbank!)*

Incidentally, a few minutes after he caught up to me and we continued on up the trail, we came to a very low-gradient pass with gorgeous panoramic views for about 300° all around us. I stopped to admire the view and take some photos, and Dad took off and left me for good.

We reached Lauenen at about 4 in the afternoon, but when we found out that there were no camping sites and the cheapest hotel was CHF 60 per person, I insisted we move on to Gsteig, where we knew there was a campground. The next leg was only 4.7 miles long and 400 yards of vertical, so we'd be done in an hour and a half, and we could always camp on the mountain if we found something suitable. Dad sat on a bench outside the Post Office, his head heavy and his eyes glazed over, silently cursing me for being a stingy bastard. After only a moment voicing his objection, however, he quietly relented and hoisted himself back up, and we continued on.

Ten minutes up the hill we realized we'd forgotten to fill up our water bottles, and although we found some reasonably flat spots, the only water source was a tiny stream the color of diarrhea. Not wanting to chance dysentery, we trudged on all the way into Gsteig, and then stumbled through the village as we struggled to locate the campground. It turned out it was situated clear across town and up a disconcertingly steep hill.

We walked 13.7 miles that day, and those final .7 were a complete bitch.

But while I was hurting, Dad was spiritually broken. It was several days before he forgave me, and weeks before I convinced him to do another tough hike. It was a Pyrrhic $100 saved, to say the least.

Tongue-napped!

Don July 12th-15th

I was mightily pissed at David for refusing to spend a few extra francs (OK, a ton of extra francs) to stay at a hotel in Lauenen. We had been on the trail for 3 weeks, and we had 6 weeks left to go. Doing what we had done that day was a good way to do permanent damage to our feet. Not to mention our desire. In any case, it was hard to tell whether we were more tired or more hungry as we trudged through Gsteig in the early evening.

The campground was half a mile up a steep hill on the other side of the town, and we briefly debated whether to stop in town to eat dinner first or walk up the hill, make camp and then come back down. Why were we eating in a restaurant rather than boiling water for another dinner of instant mashed potatoes and tuna fish? Please! As I write this, it's 4 months since we returned from our trek, and David and I both still gag at the thought.

By the way, we spent a lot of our walking time fantasizing about the food we were going to eat when we got back to the States. The Swiss government is very protective of its national agriculture, so in order to compete with the high cost of mountain-farming they place extremely high tariffs on everything they import. As such, pork and chicken (which don't take much land to farm) are the only kinds of meat you can buy for less than $40/lb. And outside of cities, ethnic or non-Swiss restaurants are not existent. So David was fixated on a ribeye steak and salmon, while my fantasies were somewhat more eclectic – spare ribs, Chinese food, Indian food, buttered popcorn, even (I'm ashamed to admit) Kentucky Fried Chicken.

When we reached the campground in Gsteig, we discovered it was in the process of deciding it didn't want to be a campground.

The owner was developing the site into a resort; the master plan was to build 20 prefab chalets, and they were going up at an incredible rate. As we were arriving that evening at 7 pm, workers were just starting to bolt walls onto a bare concrete slab. All the next day David and I watched the workers, now being assisted by two little girls who couldn't have been any more than 10 years old, throw pieces of wall and roof at the rising edifice. By 3 pm, the exterior was complete, and kitchen and bathroom fixtures were starting to disappear through the front door.

Built in a Day

The centerpiece of the resort was a brand new log building with a restaurant and the sink/toilet/shower/laundry facilities for the campground. The lounge of the restaurant was decorated in American Southwest style, which was very unusual for Switzerland, where everything tends to be done either in early Heidi or ultra-modern Office. The huge coffee table, sofas and lounge chairs were all made of rough, lacquered burl wood; the cushions of the sofas and chairs were made of un-dyed sheepskin. A big cactus sat in the center of the coffee table, and the head of a longhorn cow dolefully observed the proceedings from the wall over one of the sofas.

The Famous Swiss Longhorn – Hook 'Em

The shower room, on the other hand, was ultra-modern, Italian design, and completely non-functional. For example, there was not one clothes hook in the entire place. The only way to keep your towel and clothes off the floor and dry was to stuff them into a tiny recessed nook that was intended for some ineffectual recessed lighting.

Most of the remainder of the site was taken up with a tarmac parking lot on which half a dozen RVs were parked. Next to the restaurant was a small lawn on which two small tents were stationed. As we suspected, there was no one around that late who could tell us about camping. However, the bartender at the restaurant told us to just choose a spot and pitch our tents; someone would be by the next day to talk to us about paying.

As David and I set up our tents, we were approached by a lone British camper. He looked like a cross between Burl Ives and Santa Claus, in his early sixties with a big paunch and a short gray beard.

He was one of the most talkative people I've ever met and would kidnap (tongue-nap?) anyone who didn't know enough to avoid him. Once you were tongue-napped, you were stuck for anywhere from 10 minutes to an hour while he told you about every campsite he'd ever been in, his evaluation of the one we were staying in, every walk he'd ever done, every person he'd ever met on the trail, his job, where he lives in Yorkshire, where he used to live … . When he found out David and I were writing a book he began sharing his writing aspirations – how he'd always wanted to write a novel, but didn't have any ideas or the skill, talent, or desire to do the work. At one point he cornered David in the bathroom, which resulted in a rather uncomfortable several minutes while David smiled and nodded, hoping that if he didn't say anything eventually the guy would just shut up. It didn't work – the only thing that did was David eventually passing him off to another unsuspecting visitor by saying something like, "Hey, this guy's done some really interesting hikes around here," and then slowly backing away and avoiding eye contact as though retreating from a bear.

The tongue-napper also established himself as an inaccurate authority on every subject. He told us that there were only two restaurants in town and neither was any good, and that the campground was very expensive, charging 30 francs per person in a tent per night. We had just walked through town and seen at least four restaurants (the one we ate at later was excellent), and David and I later paid a combined total of 30 francs for the two of us for 2 nights. They must have been charging him a talking tax.

David and I got in the habit of sneaking around corners and looking ahead to make sure the tongue-napper wasn't lurking somewhere in wait. Still, in a place that tiny there was ample opportunity for him to pounce. Eventually David and I started agreeing in advance excuses that we would use to rescue each other if (when) one of us was captured.

After making camp, we went down the hill to the town to look for a restaurant, since the one on our campsite was inexplicably closed for the day. We found a charming small hotel and ordered huge meals, starting off with the enormous house special salads – lettuce, tomatoes, shredded eggs, bacon, mushrooms, cheese, and warm vinaigrette dressing. How good were they? Maybe we were overtired and suffering from a calorie-intake deficit, but halfway through the meal I noticed that we both had tears in our eyes. We went back to the same restaurant and ordered the same salads again the next night; and 5 weeks later, when we were walking north from Lugano to Zurich, we seriously considered traveling back halfway across the country to have another crack at those salads.

The entire day had been absolutely cloudless, as was the next day, which we had decided to take for foot and spirit recuperation.

Even though we were at 3,600 feet and the temperature never went above 75°F (24°C), it was uncomfortably warm to sit in direct sunlight. Not that we were ready to complain about sunshine and warmth after what we'd been through the past 3 weeks. One of the Swiss papers actually had a picture of the grounds-keepers covering the tennis courts in Gstaad because of rain at the Swiss Tennis Open; the headline read "Wimbledon in Switzerland?"

During our rest day, David and I spent 4 hours in the campground restaurant's Southwest-style lounge, with David drinking beer and the two of us starting to work on the outline of the novel that we had resolved to develop during and after the walk. By the end of that first day, the plan that we had developed was for the novel to be a murder mystery with a crusty old fart who spoke a dozen languages (all with atrocious accents), his son who was always far too eager to put himself in dangerous situations just for the hell of it, and his son's fiancée who was always blaming the father for things that weren't his fault. The key scenes would take place while they hiked together through the mountains in Switzerland. Sound familiar?

Our original plan had been to continue with the Via Alpina south into the Valais section of Switzerland and from there west to France and Mont Blanc. But from the moment we had started planning the walk, David had his heart set on going to the Montreux Jazz Festival. If we continued walking west from Gsteig, we could be there in 3 days. I had never been particularly interested in going to Montreux, and had been humoring him in the hopes that circumstances would intervene. At this point, however, the prospect of hanging out for a few days on the shore of Lac Léman listening to music sounded mighty attractive.

The next morning we bid what we expected to be a temporary farewell to the Via Alpina and headed west over the Col de Pillon to Les Diablerets, our first town in Francophone Switzerland. The whole day was warm and sunny, and the local farmers were all going crazy harvesting the hay that had been too wet to harvest for the previous month. Everyone, including me, seemed to have come down with hay fever.

It was a fairly easy walk, lots of it on road, over the *col* (the French word for "pass") and down to the bustling resort of Les Diablerets. There we checked e-mail, stocked up on groceries, and had a huge picnic lunch of salad and rotisserie chicken next to the fountain in a tiny park in the village square. We discovered that the local campground was not in Les Diablerets but in Vers l'Eglise, a 30-minute walk past Les Diablerets. *Vers l'église* means "toward the church," which created a certain amount of confusion when we were getting directions from the tourist information office. As we understood it, the agent said, "It's not in the town; it's toward the church."

"OK," I said, "where's the church?" She looked confused, and we understood her reply to be, "No, it's in the village, toward the church," when what she actually said was, "No, it's in the village, Vers l'Eglise." Eventually she showed us a map, which cleared up the confusion, and we headed out of town.

The small campground was next to a roaring stream. There was, indeed, a church in Vers l'Eglise; David and I went to a violin and organ concert there that evening. There had been some misunderstanding between the organizers and the musicians, and a few minutes after the concert was supposed to have started, the pastor of the church made an announcement in French that the organist wouldn't be there for another half hour. We were sitting behind an elderly couple from New York, who apparently couldn't speak French, because they started complaining loudly about the delay. I explained to them what the pastor had said, but they continued to make rude comments. When they wanted to say something that they didn't want David and me to understand, they would switch to Hebrew, which they spoke fairly fluently but with heavy New York accents. My Hebrew is a bit rusty, but it's good enough that I understood a lot of what they were saying. I was considering saying something to them in Hebrew on the way out after the concert, just to see how they would react, but they left early.

Although we'd eaten a camp meal before the concert, after it was over we went to a little restaurant for a second dinner. The restaurant was obscured from about shoulder height up with a blue-gray haze. I had forgotten that nearly everyone in the French-speaking world smokes Gauloise cigarettes, which as far as my nose can discern are made from dried camel dung. There were nine people besides us in the place, and 8 were smoking Gauloises; the 9th was smoking a pipe! I got very upset and told David that I wouldn't set foot in another restaurant until we were back in the U.S. That prompted a long heated argument. David put his libertarian hat on and said that there should be no no-smoking laws. And no licensing of electricians or doctors, and no health inspections of food providers. I not too politely said, "Bullshit!" I get really cranky when people smoke around me and I can't escape. *(Note from David: Dad is one of those people who feels that smokers are inherently evil people and deserve to be shot long before they have the chance to develop lung cancer. I'd like to point out that at the end of the meal we found ourselves in conversation with everyone in the restaurant, all of whom were incredibly friendly and personable.)*

Anyway, we both had fun speaking French to the locals at the campground, the church and the restaurant. It's surprising what a different mentality the Francophones have from the Teutonics. Everything moves at a much slower pace, and the buildings are certainly less well maintained. The one thing that was common was that everyone continued to be fascinated with our marathon backpacking trek. At each of the last 4 campsites we'd been given a break on the going rate after telling the proprietors our story!

The 4-hour walk from Vers l'Eglise to Aigle the next day took us 5½ hours. From the minute we left in the morning, the trail signs were terrible. Again, we were struck with the contrast to the German-speaking portion of Switzerland where, for the most part, the signs were impeccable. Several times the signs sent us in directions where the trail either petered out or ended up at a farmer's front doorstep.

At one point we had to walk on a very busy mountain road for about 2 hours. Most of the drivers were very polite and slowed down and/or gave us plenty of space. One driver, though, seemed to want to play chicken with me. It might have been because he was speeding and there was a car coming past in the other direction just as he reached me, so he couldn't move over. In any case, he came past me with no more than 12 inches to spare. As he passed, I hit the side of his car as hard as I could with my trekking pole. I was waiting for him to stop and yell at me so I could shove the pole down his throat, but he just sped on. It was a stupid thing to have done, since the pole was on a strap around my wrist; if it had gotten caught on something it would have ripped my arm off. A minute later I noticed that the rubber tip of that pole was missing. The force of the blow must have torn it off. I would have to buy a replacement, but I decided it had been worth it.

We found a lovely campground on the outskirts of Aigle, a vineyard town on the Rhône River about 10 miles upstream from Lac Léman. A few miles away on the other side of the valley we could see the mountains of France.

A final note on facial hair before I let David take us to Montreux. Both David and I stopped shaving the day we left the U.S. In my case, it meant that by this time I had quite an acceptable full gray beard. In David's case, it meant that he had the barest shadow of a moustache on his upper lip and half a dozen scraggly whiskers on his chin. But was he proud of those few whiskers! Whenever we were near some place that had a mirror, he would preen and boast about how awesome his beard looked. I would allow as how I seemed to be winning the beard-growing contest, at which he'd get very offended ... . But I guess I'll let him tell you his side of the story.

Lakeward Bound

David   July 15th-18th

When I found out that Dad was writing letters back home gloating about how he was winning the beard-growing contest I was completely shocked. You have to wonder what it says about him that he has to compete with a 26-year-old in a facial hair growing contest in order to feel better about himself. Nevertheless I felt forced to defend my honor. While it is true that I could not compete in terms of quantity, in terms of quality I was the clear victor, since my facial hair made me look like a 17th century French nobleman while his made him look like a hobo.

In looking back at photos of myself at the end of the trip, I can't help but recoil in horror at how awful I actually looked. The chin scruff was silly, but the "moustache" was just embarrassing. I can't believe he let me be seen in public like that.

Except for Elm, which was a single municipal campsite in the woods rather than a serviced campground, the price of camping in Aigle was half as much as the next cheapest place we'd been. Welcome to the flatlands, where the air is thick, the temperature constant, and hot water and electricity are just a little easier to come by. We also noticed we'd made it into wine country. Whereas cows cover the landscape most everywhere in Switzerland, here in the canton of Vaud we saw mostly vineyards as far as the eye could see. Everywhere we looked there were grapevines impeccably organized (much like everything else in Switzerland), with tall stalks but small grapes, thanks to the exceedingly high rain-to-sun ratio this season had brought.

Having spent 4 weeks in the mountains, we were about ready for a change of pace, and were excited to be only a few hours' walk from Lac Léman (Lake Geneva). Spending a few days lounging around on the lake sounded wonderful, so after setting up camp we walked into town to see if we could find information on trails, campgrounds, and ways we might be able to amuse ourselves for the next few days. We discovered it was Sunday (you start to lose track of time after 4 weeks on vacation), which meant the only thing we found open was a döner kebab restaurant. But we were happy to come back in the morning, since we'd have to walk through town to head toward the lake anyway.

I told the agent at the tourist information office (in French) of our plans to walk to Lac Léman, and he asked me to repeat my sentence, because he hadn't understood. I repeated it, and he corrected my pronunciation of "Léman." Funny, as awful as Dad's French accent is (he was always elated when someone responded to him in French rather than just running away screaming), I'm the one who gets corrected. Frankly I think the guy was just a dickhead – it takes a serious willful negligence not to catch the name of a major geographic landmark 3 miles away from you, even in a language in which every word sounds the same.

Before Dad chimes in to defend himself, I should point out that French is a language he's never had a lesson in. He taught himself entirely from books and tapes, and actually reads better than I do. It's just that when he tries to say, *Merci beaucoup* (thank you very much) it comes out *Merci, beau cul* (thank you, nice ass).

Our tourist information clerk showed us the trails that would lead us to the lake, and the schedule of events for the Montreux Jazz Festival, informing us that almost everything was free, except for the really big concerts. We delighted in that and scampered on our merry way toward the Swiss Rhône[13], which we would be following to its mouth at Lake Geneva.

We had a bit of a hard time finding the trail. For a while we

---

[13] The Rhône originates in the Swiss Alps and then flows into Lake Geneva. It comes out the other end as the famous French Rhône, heading to Lyon and then south into the Mediterranean.

walked along a hike-and-bike path next to a drainage ditch, and once even lost that and had to climb down from a bridge and through some briars to pick it up again. We wondered idly whether this was the Rhône (knowing it couldn't possibly be) or if we'd managed to miss it somewhere. It seemed unlikely – according to our map, all roads lead to the Rhône,[14] and given the quantity of rainfall one would expect the largest river in that part of Switzerland to be wider than 6 feet. At the same time it felt like we'd walked much further west than we should have.

And then, suddenly, there it was – 150 feet wide, the largest, most majestic body of rushing dirty brown water this side of the Mississippi. There was no mistaking it, and we followed it downstream to where the brown of the mountain silt disappears into the gorgeous clear blue water of Lake Geneva.

We spent the night in a town called Le Bouveret, in a campground with thousands of vacationers packed in like battery-farmed chickens. Le Bouveret has a recently-built aquapark (which we considered visiting until we saw the prices) and a number of privately owned beaches, one of which we received free admission to, courtesy of our campground.

I walked over to the beach with my notebook and sat on a rock, looking around for bare female breasts, as one does on beaches in Europe. I was surprised by two things. First, how impossible it was to tell how old some of these women were. Everyone, without exception, was uncompromisingly beautiful, and the best I could do to guess at people's ages was offer some sort of vague estimate of whether they were closer to 16 or to 60. Beyond that, it was incredibly tough.

The second thing that surprised me was the distinct lack of naked breastage. It had been a week since I'd seen Angela and I was

---

[14] Funny story. As I'm sure you've gathered by now, Dad is really into puns, and he came up with this one as a weak pun on the phrase "All roads lead to Rome." While we were editing the book, though, Dad changed this phrase to read "all the streams in that area ..." because he forgot his own pun. As we say in French, "Quel dork-monkey."

starting to feel desperate, and what began as eager anticipation turned into violent depression as I realized there wasn't a single pair of topless tits on the entire beach. What kind of beach was this, anyway? Even the beaches in Holland have bare tits galore, and it's freezing there all the time. The only girls in Le Bouveret who were topless were the ones younger than 10 and, thank you, that's not my cup of tea. I was relieved, though not entirely satisfied, when one woman changed into her street clothes at the end of the afternoon and exposed herself for a few seconds in the process. The rest of the time, I just moped.

Dad joined me at the beach after a while and then left as I stayed to close out the evening. I wrote a poem in French:

> Les jeuns et les vieux
> S'assoient sur le vert de la plage.
> Ils se levent, ici l'un, ici l'autre
> Et quittent la scène.
> L'annonceur a dit merci et au revoir
> Et veuillez revenir à demain.
> Nous ne reviendrons pas demain.
> Nous quittons cette ville
> Et voyagons encore, ici à l'un, ici à l'autre
> Et disons merci et au revoir,
> Jamais y voire encore.'

Translation:

> The young and the old
> Sit on the green of the beach,
> They rise, first one, then another
> And leave the scene.
> The announcer has said thank you and goodbye
> And please come back tomorrow.
> We won't come back tomorrow
> We leave this town
> And travel some more, first to one, then to another
> And say thank you and goodbye
> Never to see them again.

I wrote some prose, too:

> As the world left for dinner, for games, for evening activities, I sat and watched the sunset in all its glorious beauty, the softest waves licking gingerly at the sand in front of me, the sun now further away and with more atmosphere to fight through, sneaking behind clouds and peeking out only rarely, instead sending rays of light straight up through the sky and creating a personal ceiling of magnificent glory, so tranquil, so elusive, and so subtle.

> A seagull of some variety skimmed across the surface of the water in search of food. Coming up short it re-ascended, disappeared behind a bluff, and then circled back to look for more. Others, off in the distance, did the same. The clouds on the horizon flattened in my eyes.

The mosquitoes began attacking. The families all departed and a new crowd arrived – mostly teenagers smoking pot and drinking beer. A pair of swans approached a couple of Dutch guys sitting on the sand with a bong. The guys backed off, and one tried to scare the birds away – running at them, yelling at them, and approaching them with a bottle of cologne which he tried to spray in the swans' faces. Obviously this guy didn't know what I knew, thanks to my 6 years at TASIS, that swans are **not to be taunted!** Fortunately the beasts decided not to break any of his bones and after a few minutes they returned to the water and swam away.

For the second straight night I had a hard time sleeping, sweating constantly because my sleeping bag was far too heavy for the heat of sea-level summertime camping. In the morning, feeling like hens liberated from the huge chicken coop of "battery" camping, Dad and I set out on the short walk through Les Grangettes to Villeneuve.

In case you were wondering, Les Grangettes comes from a French phrase meaning "Swampland of a Billion Mosquitos, You Will Die of Exsanguination Face Down in the Mud." Not really, but trust me, visiting in the summer is not a good idea.

As we started off we passed an old Swiss French couple who were wearing ankle high slippers in what was increasingly muddy terrain. The mud became a swampy bog, and as we entered the forest we were suddenly surrounded by literally millions of mosquitoes. Whichever of us was behind could see them swarming toward us, presumably attracted by the smell of the person in front. For 20 minutes we held our hats in our hands and swatted mercilessly at every exposed inch of our bodies – our legs, our arms, our faces, our necks, our arms, our ears, our legs, our faces, our ears, our arms, our necks, our legs, and so on. For the first time on the trip our arms were getting as much exercise as our legs. We wondered what became of the couple we'd passed, and hoped they'd been smart enough to turn around and run, because damn, this was vampirical. If ever there was a place on the planet that needed more frogs and bats, this was it. You could die of mosquito bites in territory like this.

We emerged from the forest to a campsite, which was no doubt owned and patronized only by suicidal morons. We continued on through more mosquito-ridden swampland and into Villeneuve, walked though the old town, and quickly found the tourist information office where we asked for a campground, *sans moustiques* (without mosquitos). The lady wasn't much help in the moustiques-free department, but showed us where the campgrounds were, and we made a beeline for the one furthest away from the swampland from which we had just emerged.

Now here's a pop quiz for you: other than humans, what do mosquitoes eat? We realized, after the whole thing was over, that we hadn't seen a single lifeform in that entire swamp other than us, and as many billions of mosquitoes as there were, what could they possibly be eating? We began to get incredibly curious, and lamented for the umpteenth time that the thing we missed most through all of this was not toilets or processed foods or a warm bed with a pillow and a blanket, but the lack of constant Internet accessibility. At least three or four times a day we'd come up with a question that begged being looked up on the Internet, but when you're only coming to an Internet terminal once every 3 or 4 days (at best), there's a tendency to forget what those questions are.

This question – what mosquitoes eat when they're not eating mammals – was one of the only ones that survived the entire 2-month journey and that we looked up later. It turns out they don't rely on blood for sustenance at all – they're nectar feeders, much like bees or gnats, and the females (and females only) drink blood when they're pregnant for a tasty extra protein treat.

So in case you needed any more encouragement, if you see a mosquito biting you, go ahead and kill it – because the bitch has whole bakery in the oven.

After lunch we decided we'd rent some bicycles and cycle around the lake. After all, we'd only walked a few miles in the past couple of days, and I was starting to feel a little lethargic. The rental process was far more of a chore than it should have been. The guy attending the only bike shop in town was obviously a mechanic and not a businessman, and every question we asked required him going upstairs to ask his mother the answer. "Can we rent the bikes for 24 hours, rather than 8 am to 5 pm?"

"Hold on, I'll check." Clump, clump, clump, clump, clump. Pause. Clump, clump, clump, clump.

"Yes."

"How much is that going to cost?"

"Um ... Hold on." Clump, clump, clump, clump, clump.

When we abandoned that alternative as being just too darned complicated and decided to rent the cycles for 4 hours, he had trouble figuring out what time we should return them, since a quarter-to-one plus 4 hours is really tough math. Eventually we got ourselves onto the road and cycled to Montreux, Vevey (Nestle's world headquarters), and Saint-Saphorin before turning around and heading back the way we'd come.

I'd made up my mind early on that we would visit the world's number one *fête du jazz* – and indeed, when we had begun planning the trip months in advance, the famous festival had played at least some part in our itinerary. Our initial, rather over-ambitious dream of spending 6 months walking the entire Via Alpina required starting in Monaco and high-tailing it so we could catch the last few days of Montreux while we were "in the area" (it would be roughly 40 miles away, but that's closer than it would be from Texas, anyway). As the scale of our trip became less grand, Montreux continued to play at least into the back of my mind, and any time we pulled out maps and looked at our long-term trajectory I'd bring it up. Dad would usually just nod and smile, since he wasn't that interested and didn't see why I was. But here we were, cycling through Montreux right smack in the middle of the festival's 3-week timeframe.

As we passed through the city, we came upon an outdoor bandshell and sat for a couple of hours listening to the bands. The most amazing thing about the Montreux Jazz Festival, other than the musicians, is that it's one of the most outstandingly low-income-friendly events on the planet. Between the Under The Sky Festival, the competitions, the lectures, the workshops, and the films, there are so many free activities, you could, in theory, stay there for the entire festival and spend no money except on food and a place to sleep. If you camped and went into town to buy groceries, you could do that for about $300 a week. The only thing that costs are the feature acts, many of whom don't even play jazz (in 1995 I saw Ice T there, and this year's lineup included Motorhead, the Beastie Boys, Tori Amos, Prince, and Wu Tang Clan). Of course you'll have to pay out the wazoo for food, drinks and souvenirs if you decide to patronize the Montreux Jazz Café or spend too much time hanging around the stalls surrounding the music venues. That being said, the food stalls have ethnic foods from all over the world that look and smell unbelievably good.

Dad and I had so much fun that we decided we'd come back the next day, and in the late afternoon we returned to the campground, where we had dinner and I once again spent the evening by the lake sitting, writing, and staring at the water. While sitting on a bench, I was approached by a gentleman named Ernest, who was roughly my Dad's age and wearing a bikini bottom, which is an unfortunate tradition among European men. Ernest was from Basel, a city in northwest Switzerland right on the German border and 20 miles from the French border. He was very well-traveled, having lived or toured extensively all over Europe, Scandinavia, the U.S., and Australasia.

We enjoyed a very nice conversation. I talked about walking across Switzerland; he talked about sex. I talked about how nasty mosquitoes are; he talked about sex. I asked him what the French word for "swan" was; he asked me if I'd ever had sex with a man. I talked about where Angela and I wanted to go for our honeymoon; he told me how wonderful New Zealand is, we should definitely go there for our honeymoon, and would I like to join him in caravan #9?

I declined his invitation, and we continued to talk about things like sex. Eventually the sun dropped, the mosquitoes started attacking, and I got up to take my leave. Ernest told me that if I wanted a blowjob I knew where to find him. I thanked him, returned to camp and immortalized him in my journal.

The next day we walked back to Montreux, stopping along the way at the Château de Chillon, the most visited castle in Switzerland, made famous by Lord Byron in the poem "Prisoner of Chillon." Because of the poem and the fact that Byron etched his name on one of the dungeon pillars, it's often thought that he spent time there as an involuntary guest. In fact, he was a tourist like us, but was inspired by the story of a bishop who had been imprisoned there and, unlike us, wrote a poem about it that made him world famous.[15] We were given a tour by a woman who looked and sounded like Edna from *The Incredibles.*

We then continued on to Montreux, where we spent the day listening to some of the best jazz musicians from around the world, musicians I otherwise never would have had the opportunity to hear, musicians from places like ... Texas.

No joke. After traveling 6,000 miles and walking across Switzerland, the July 17th feature artist was Norah Jones (from Dallas) and in the "Under the Sky" outdoor stage the next day, the opening acts were the Texas State University (TSU) Salsa Del Rio Band and the TSU Jazz Ensemble, located in San Marcos, roughly half an hour's drive south of Austin.

We did, however, get to witness the finals of the solo piano competition, whose participants were from France, Austria, Azerbaijan, and Cuba. It was some of the most extraordinary piano playing I've ever heard in my life, though it's interesting how, when you're in this kind of situation you have to be so nitpicky in order to make your choice for the Audience Favorite Award. After some of the comments I've made about Ballet Austin and the Austin Symphony Orchestra, Angela has said she'll never let me witness her playing the cello.[16] But the ability to identify where synchronicity, rhythm, and percussiveness aren't spot on is a pretty good skill to have. Sometimes I feel guilty judging people like this – after all, the only songs I can play on the piano are "Romeo and Juliet" and Richard Marx's "Right Here Waiting," and even those I can't play with anything resembling synchronicity, rhythm, or percussiveness.

---

[15] I should try that:

O Prisoner of Chillon!

I am overcome with emotion

I must put to paper my pen,

As you put to the dungeon pillar your knife ... or fingernail, or whatever you use to carve your name.

O! The doggerel ... the doggerel.

[16] On a related note, you should take a moment to go to YouTube and search for "Pachelbel Rant". Trust me on this one.

However, we had to vote for who we thought should receive the audience award, and I'm a judgmental prick anyway.

The Austrian, a guy named David Helbock, was far and away the most creative of the musicians, but the weakest technically. The Frenchman was better technically, but lacked creativity, the Azerbaijani was technically superior but lacked personality, and the Cuban, Rolando Luna Carrillo had it all. He won the top prize and the audience award, and played us out with an encore that … well, wasn't quite as good. But again, we're talking about minutia among four of the best up-and-coming musicians on the planet.

At that point Dad caught the (free!) bus back to Villeneuve, while I decided to hang out to catch some more Jazz Under the Sky. The sun was setting, and by the time I made it back to the stage, the night crowd had come in – drunk and high teenagers – while the band on stage was no longer jazz but was now death metal. I quickly tired of the atmosphere, so I found an Internet terminal where I spent an hour writing to friends and family and then headed back to camp.

France – Lac Léman to Mont Blanc

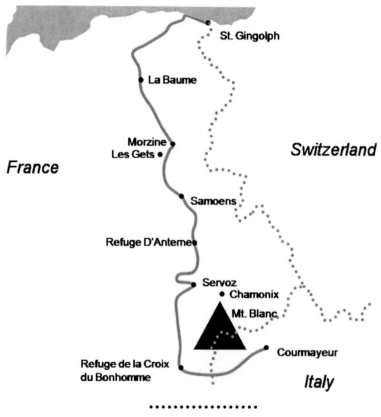

David's Search for Naked Breastage

Don   **July 19th-20th**

The next morning we planned to continue our walk west, so we packed up and went into town to figure out how to get back to Le Bouveret without subjecting ourselves to Les Grangettes, home to Satan's vampire-spawn. We had just missed a ferry and the next one wasn't for 2 hours, so we went to the bus station to see when the next bus was. There were no buses to Le Bouveret, so we were told to go to the train station. The guy at the train station ticket counter showed us a route we could take, which involved three transfers and would get us there 7 minutes later than the next ferry would. So we stocked up on groceries, had a picnic lunch in a park along the waterfront, and then took the ferry to Le Bouveret. Being in the wind on the water was a relief from the heat of the past several days.

From Le Bouveret we walked on a busy road along the lakefront to St. Gingolph, which is on the border, half in Switzerland and half in France. Along the way, David continually scanned the shore for bare breasts. The lack of topless sunbathers had apparently been an extensive topic of conversation between him and Ernest 2 nights before. Ernest had assured him that once we were in France, the views would get better. Sure enough, a few hundred yards before the border, David's efforts were rewarded. After a few minutes of him standing there staring while pretending not to be staring, I dragged him away to continue our journey. (Sure, they were nice, but it wasn't as though they could tap dance.)

At the border we were all ready with our passports, but nobody seemed interested, so we just walked across the frontier into France. We went into the local tourist information office to get some advice on the GR (Grand Route) 5, one of the European long-distance walking trails, which heads south from St. Gingolph to Mont Blanc. However, where the Swiss tourist office personnel had always been very knowledgeable and encouraging about hiking and backpacking, the agent at the French St. Gingolph tourist office seemed to think the whole thing was impossible and beyond the comprehension of man. After the first full day's walk south (which David and I had estimated would take us a couple of hours) we would enter the unknown. He didn't know if there were any mountain huts or any places to buy food, and he certainly didn't know how long it would take us to get to where civilization again became available.

Every time we asked him a question he would say he couldn't help us. As we left, we thanked him for trying and he said, "À votre service," (At your service). It reminded me of a story from when I was teaching English as a Foreign Language in Tehran in 1974. At lunchtime, my teaching colleagues and I used to frequent a small restaurant across the street from the school. Our usual waiter, a dapper young man who was always dressed in a suit, did his best for us, but the restaurant was constantly out of everything on the menu. It got to be a standing joke, so we made up a simulated ordering session in Farsi that went something like this:

"I'll have the meat kebab."

"I'm sorry, we don't have meat kebab today."

"OK, then I'll have the chicken kebab."

"We're all out of chicken kebab."

"Then I'll have the lentil stew."

"We don't have any lentil stew."

"What do you have?"

"We don't have anything."

"Then bring me the bill."

"At your service."

Up until that point, the information we had gotten from the Via Alpina website had always been sufficient to let us know what was coming. We were planning on rejoining the Via Alpina in Samöens, about a 2-day walk north of Chamonix and Mont Blanc. As near as we could figure, that should take us about 4 days. But as David and I stood outside the tourist information office in St. Gingolph, it was clear to us that we needed to rethink our plan. The flat area by the lakeshore was only a hundred yards wide. From there, the mountains went up nearly vertically up and disappeared quickly into the clouds. Heading up there without understanding what was going to happen next seemed like a terrible idea.

From the information we had managed to pry out of the information office, it looked as though if we headed west along the lake road for another 15 miles toward Evian *(Note from David: I visited Evian when I was 15, and there were lots of naked breasts)*, the mountains to the south of us would level off to a high plateau sprinkled with farming villages. It seemed like a much better idea to walk over that plateau and from there up one of the valleys into the mountains of Haute Savoy than to head up into the unknown. Eventually, of course, we would have to get up and over the last ridges before reaching Chamonix and Mont Blanc, but we'd worry about that when we came to it.

The next several hours walking west along the road were, frankly, miserable. It was hot and humid, the road was very busy and very narrow, and there was little or no shoulder. The only excitement was that David spotted a couple skinny dipping a few yards off shore. Give it a rest, kid.

Eventually, as he was wont to do every hour or so, David announced that he was starving and had to eat NOW! We found a small road that led down to a rocky public beach and walked down to the shore. It was 6 pm, and there were about 10 people on the beach. Over the next half hour, while we ate, all but one couple left. At that point, the thunderstorm that had been threatening us all day decided to break and the last couple fled. We quickly went to the far end of the beach and set up our tents on the rocks where we couldn't be seen from the road. In between thundershowers, we went swimming in the lake (where we rinsed out our sweaty clothes) and cooked dinner.

We had a pretty good idea that we weren't supposed to be camping there. But by 9 pm it had gotten dark and the thundershowers were continuing, so we thought we had an excellent chance of making it through the night without someone coming to chase us off or arrest us.

When I got up to take my 2 am pee, the haze had cleared and I had a fantastic view of the lights on the other side of the lake from Lausanne to Montreux.

A Funny Thing Happens ...

David   **July 20th**

A funny thing happens when you've been backpacking for a month. When you stop, your body continues to produce all that adrenalin and doesn't know what to do with it. You start to get anxious. You get nervous. Your mind starts racing and you have trouble sleeping. When you hop on the trail or a treadmill and hammer out a few miles you feel miraculously cured for about a day, and then your mind slowly starts to spiral into disquiet again. It's an addiction, much like heroin, and you just need your fix.

I'd experienced this kind of thing before. In September 2005 I completed an Olympic distance triathlon (1,500m swim, 40k bike, 10k run), and immediately afterward my brother and I began training for a marathon. For 11 months straight I'd exercised 5-10 hours a week. And then, the day after the marathon, I stopped. No more jumping into outdoor swimming pools in the dark and the rain; no more waking up at 6 am for mile repeats in the biting cold; no more 3-hour runs on the weekends or 10.1-mile loops of the Town Lake Hike and Bike Trail; no more diving into Barton Springs to cool ourselves off after 15 miles in the sun. At first it was a tremendous relief, and I was glad to be done with it. But almost immediately I got so nervous and anxious that I constantly felt as though my head was going to explode.

This is what had happened to me over the past couple of days and was why I'd insisted we take a long bike ride on the day we'd arrived in Villeneuve. It had happened earlier on this trip, too. On the drive back from Zurich I'd mentioned how anxious I was. We'd been idle for 2 days and my leg was starting to twitch. Dad had already warned me once or twice that it would happen, that my body would start to associate accomplishment with walking 10 miles over a mountain ridge with 35 pounds on my back, but from that moment on he wouldn't let up. I suppose after a month of 24-hour contact with someone you run out of things to talk about, but I got really fed up with him bombarding me daily with warnings about how depressed I would be, as though he was wishing it on me. I told him to cut it out, but there was no doubt he was right.

During our sun-filled days on Lac Léman I was starting to go insane. In my defense, I loved the day we spent at Montreux and I hated the day we walked into France, so it wasn't entirely exercise-related. There were a number of factors contributing to the overall level of my misery. First was the heat, to which we had clearly become unaccustomed. Beach-bumming is a notoriously lethargic activity, and the kind of muscle-tired that comes from a day of hiking is very different than the kind of soul-suckingly head-tired you get from a day of sunbathing. Second was the fact that much of our walking for the past week had been on paved roads, which are far harder on the feet and more apt to cause blisters, and make your joints sore at an alarming rate. That explains the day we walked through St. Gingolph.

Third was the mosquitoes. Mosquitoes like standing water and warm, humid environments. Most of the Swiss mountains don't qualify; the environs of Lac Léman do. Even aside from our swampland experience in Les Grangettes, we were really getting sick of having to seal ourselves in our tents every night to keep from being eaten alive.

And fourth was the people, who were almost as ubiquitous as the mosquitoes and far, far more obnoxious. Aside from the loud, impersonal nature of the campsite at Le Bouveret, the obnoxious New Yorkers at Vers l'Eglise, and the jam-packed beaches, perhaps the worst violation was when we stopped at an Intermarché grocery store in Maxilly the morning after sleeping on the rock beach. We were there early in the morning, and at the entrance there was an African immigrant setting up a table with sunglasses, wallets, belts, and other assorted accessories. I was in the market for some sunglasses, so I stopped to look at his display. He glared at me and asked me what I wanted, obviously annoyed that I was interrupting him in the middle of setting up his table. I asked him what the prices were. He stared at me with contempt. It was the same look I used to give my parents when they told me to take out the trash while I was in the middle of playing Nintendo – "How dare you inconvenience me at a time like this?!"

He answered, "They're sunglasses. They're for the sun." That, of course, is the answer to the question, "What are these?" not the question I had asked, which was, "What are the prices?"

"Oui, je comprends," I said, "quels sont les prix?" (Yes, I understand, what are the prices?)

He asked me which pair I was looking at, and I randomly pointed to one. "Huit francs," he said, "Eight," and then he held up eight fingers. I picked the pair up and tried them on, and he gave me a mirror, but by now I was so turned off by his attitude that I wasn't even remotely interested in doing business with him. I took the pair off and put them back on the table, and as I turned to walk away he half-slapped, half-pushed me on the side of the head, angry that I dared waste his time.

At the time I was too stunned to do anything, but as soon as we walked out the door I regretted not punching him in the face. In retrospect I'm glad I didn't – he outweighed me by a good 70 lbs. Nonetheless, I was so angry that he treated me like that, it put me in a foul mood for the next hour.

During that hour we had started climbing into the hills, and got lost because French trail blazes are easily confused with smudges of moss on trees. We came upon an old man talking to someone in front of his house, and when we asked him for directions, he spent fifteen minutes with us, making sure we knew exactly where we were going, how to get there, and which detours we'd come to that we didn't want to take.

And there you have it – the classic difference between city folk – who never have time for anyone – and country folk – who have more than enough time for everyone. It was good to be back in the mountains again.

In a Sardine Can a Mile Above Sea Level

Don   **July 20th-25th**

We quickly climbed from 1,155 feet, the altitude of the lake, to 2,800 feet and the town of St. Paul en Chablais. There we found a tiny grocery store that had a large-scale map of all the territory we'd be walking through for the next 3 days. We purchased it with relief. We also bought a half-dozen eggs, some turkey-ham, some shredded Emmenthaler cheese and a baguette for our first cooked breakfast meal in a month. The thunderstorm that had been chasing us all morning finally caught us, and we took shelter under the roof of an information kiosk next to the town hall to cook our fantastic meal. As you can imagine, any kind of food other than peanut butter and jelly on crackers or things you dissolved in boiling water was cause for celebration by this point in the trip.

By the time we finished, the sun had come out. We maneuvered on trails and small roads gently uphill and across the plateau, rarely finding trail markings that served us for more than about a quarter of a mile at a time, but greatly assisted by the new map. We had intended to stop at a campground in the town of Vinzier, but we made much faster time than we expected and decided to press on into the high valleys to the next campground, which we estimated to be about 2½ hours walk away.

We could take a trail or walk alongside the road to the next village, La Vernaz. The style of dotted line on the map showing the trail was identified in the key as meaning "Maybe it will be there and maybe it won't." But roads are hard on the feet, and David was sick of walking on them, so we took the trail. It gave out after a few minutes and we spent about 40 minutes scrambling in stream beds and up steep, densely forested hillsides, before finally coming back to the road, which led us to a well-marked trail, which took us to La Vernaz. By this time it was pouring again, and we had no choice but to plod on the road downhill in the rain to the campground at La Baume.

La Baume is in a valley surrounded by ski resorts, and the campground is run by the municipality of La Baume to encourage tourism during the summer. We'd been worried about getting there late and maybe finding it full, but when we arrived we found the loneliest woman in southeastern France – Madame Catherine Coffy – at the reception hut. Catherine, a perennially cheerful and helpful woman in her mid-30s, works in the local school. The municipality keeps her on in the summer to manage the campground. There were 25 huge, beautifully flat camping places, each separated from the others by high, thick hedges; all but two of them were vacant. We told Catherine our story about walking for 2 months, and she gave us a discount, as we were starting to expect. The fee was €8.60[17], about $12.00, or about two-thirds of the cheapest price we'd paid anywhere in Switzerland. We hoped that the price differential would continue. The showers were free, which was virtually unheard of at the campsites in Switzerland, though they were the kind that shut off automatically every 15 seconds, and you have to push the button again to get the water back on. Kind of like a trained rat working for food pellets.

We took the next day as a tourism and foot recuperation day. David and I took the bus a mile back up the road to see the Gorge du Pont du Diable (the Gorge of the Devil's Bridge), an impressive chasm formed by the Dranse de Morzine. At some time in antiquity a huge rock fell over the chasm, creating a natural bridge, which the natives had used for thousands of years to get from one side of the

---

[17] € is the symbol for Euros, the common currency for much of the European Union. When it was introduced in January 2002, the first letters of the countries which adopted the Euro spelled the words "BAFFLING PIGS." Six years and 12 countries later, 9 of which are not even in the European Union, the best acronym they can come up with is LLANSSBICHPFFIGGBLECSSPERM, which is rumored to be Welsh for "Angry sheep telling farmer, 'Back off, Bucko!'"

river to the other. Over time, the river dug a 150-foot canyon underneath the bridge, and they've now fastened stairs and walkways throughout the Gorges so people can experience the awesome current below them continuing to carve away at the surrounding rocks.

Incidentally, the bus ride cost us €1 (about $1.40) each. Two hours later, when we took the bus in the other direction, the driver insisted on not taking any additional fare and we rode the 14 miles to Les Gets at the other end of the valley for free.

In case the price difference hadn't been evidence enough, the punctuality (or lack of it) of the bus service gave us proof that we weren't in Switzerland any more. We were waiting outside the gift shop at the gorge for the scheduled arrival of the bus when it pulled up around 15 minutes early. The driver stood talking to a colleague for about 5 minutes and then the two of them walked a hundred yards down the road and disappeared into a bar. (I hoped he was getting a soft drink, but I suspect he wasn't.) Ten minutes passed, then 15.

Finally, 5 minutes after the bus was supposed to have left, the driver and his friend came out of the bar. A few minutes after that, the driver opened the door, we and the other waiting passengers boarded the bus, and we started our journey.

We rode the bus to Les Gets, a ski town high up at the south end of the valley. Ski resorts often try to think of creative ways to drum up business in the summer, and the popular pastime here can only be described as extreme mountain biking. People get dressed up in full body armor, take souped-up bicycles with industrial strength shock-absorbers up the cable car, and then barrel down the mountain at 60 miles an hour. The whole town was filled with people covered in plastic body armor and mud. It looked like a scene from one of the *Mad Max* movies.

While David and I were eating lunch at an outdoor table at a restaurant, two bikers rode up, stripped off their armor, and sat down at the next table. They started talking to each other and I began my favorite game of eavesdropping to see if I could understand what they were saying, or at least identify whatever language they were speaking. At first, I was sure it was one of the Scandinavian languages; I was leaning toward Danish because one of the guys was swallowing all his consonants. But every now and then he sounded like he was speaking Dutch. Except the words weren't Dutch, which I would definitely have recognized, since Dutch is one of my strongest languages. I listened more and was starting to think it was a dialect of Frisian or something exotic like that. When I went off to the men's room David struck up a conversation with them and asked them where they were from. It turned out that they were speaking Norwegian, but the one that was perplexing me was from Holland and was speaking Norwegian with a heavy Dutch accent. So I allowed myself to think I had kept my game average up and my pride intact.

Les Gets also has a museum with the largest collection of mechanical musical instruments in Europe – music boxes, street organs, orchestrions, that sort of thing. When we lived in the Netherlands in the late 1970s and early 1980s, the nearby city of Utrecht had a similar museum. I remembered it as a wonderful place to visit, and going to the Museum of Mechanical Music was the primary reason for our trip to Les Gets. We've all seen and heard player pianos, music boxes and street organs, but violins, clarinets and trumpets that play themselves are something else altogether.

When we got back to the campsite, it started to rain heavily, so David and I took shelter under the eaves of the reception hut and struck up a conversation with Catherine. As I said, things were not really busy at La Baume campground, and she clearly welcomed the company. Before long she had opened a bottle of wine and a box of tomatoes and cut up a sausage roll. She phoned her husband who drove over from their nearby house, and we spent the next 2 hours drinking and eating and discussing politics and employment and laws and customs (all in French). What a gas! It was nice to learn that they are as skeptical of what their government has done to France in the past 10 years as we are of our current presidential leadership.

After Catherine and her husband left, a torrential downpour continued for the rest of the night.

The next day dawned clear and warm, and we had a pleasant walk up the valley from La Baume to Morzine. By now David had become exceedingly skeptical of walking on roads, and he started out insisting that we take an 80-minute hike on a trail rather than a 10-minute walk on the road to get to the same point. I eventually managed to talk some sense into him, and after that first 10 minutes most of the rest was in level forest on both sides of the Dranse de Morzine.

About half way, we passed through a tiny hamlet where a bright-eyed old man sat watching us from his front porch. "Is this your first time walking by here?" he asked us in French.

"Yes," we replied. Like a flash he was down his steps and pointing to a mountain formation in the direction from which we had come.

"What does that look like?" he asked us.

"I don't know," I replied.

"Do you see the elephant? There is the forehead, and there's the trunk, and those are the ears and the tusks." He extended his arm and stroked the air in the shape of the trunk and tusks.

"Yes," we replied, getting excited. "That's fantastic."

Next, he told us that it is 1,150 km (720 miles) from there to England. He told us about a local relay team that ran in half hour shifts day and night from there to England and wanted me to guess how long it took them. I guessed 5 days, and he gleefully told me that it was only four. In all, we chatted with him for about 10 minutes. He was so pleased at our responses to everything he had to say, that when we left his face was beaming. Parked at the side of his house was a small food-stand truck that said, "Tom Pizza," and we wondered whether this exuberant old man, well into his eighties, was Tom, never having retired because he just loved his job, giving people the pleasure of pizza. Regardless, I'm sure we made his day, and I know he made ours.

As we were approaching Morzine, I told David we should fork off the road and go to a campground that I had seen the day before in the suburb of Montriond on our bus ride to Les Gets. He insisted that there would be lots better campgrounds in Morzine, and that we should go to the tourist information office in the center of town. When we got there, it turned out that there were only two campgrounds in the area, one of which was the one I'd wanted to go to, and the other was also a mile and a half back in the direction from which we'd come. We decided to go back to the one in Montriond.

One cultural note that I haven't yet told you is that nearly all businesses in rural Switzerland and France (other than restaurants) close for several hours in the middle of the day: 11:30-2:00, 12:00-2:30, those kinds of hours. We were frequently in need of supplies when we walked through towns during those hours and would either have to make do without them or sit and wait until the stores opened again. We arrived in Morzine at 12:45 and needed to buy a map for our next stages, but we had to sit and cool our heels for nearly 2 hours until something opened. But that was OK, because we sat on a bench and had a delicious lunch of … peanut butter and jelly on crackers.

In deference to the "extreme biking" industry, which was even more prominent in Morzine than it had been in Les Gets, the campground in Montriond had a bike wash facility. It was in constant use all evening. As we'd walked through Morzine, we had walked by half a dozen bike rental shops, and there had been hundreds of muddy, armored people riding through town on their way to or from the ski lifts.

We had a tough 7½-hour walk the next day. It started up the trails next to the ski lift leaving Morzine, and since they were all being used by cyclists, we had to be on constant lookout to avoid getting run down. The trees around the trail all had bright orange pads to reduce the mortality rate from people crashing into them all day long. (The mortality rate of the people, probably not the trees.) At one point David was crossing the trail and came within a half second of getting annihilated by a cyclist careening downhill around a bend at 30 miles per hour. As David dove out of the way, we heard the cyclist's fading voice shout, "Merci!"

There were dozens of ski lifts all around as we made our way to the top of the Col de Joux Plane. For the last 45 minutes of the ascent we could see at the top of the valley a U-shaped ridge from which we would get our first view of Mont Blanc 4 days' walk to the south. We crested the ridge to find a group of French hikers strewn on and around a rustic bench, staring at a distant cloudbank.

"Mont Blanc?" inquired David.

"Should be," replied one of the hikers.

"That storm will be here in a couple of hours," added another.

David and I looked at each other, shrugged our shoulders, and walked on, first along the top of the ridge and then for 4 hours steeply down the other side of the col in the face of an increasingly powerful wind and intermittent rain showers.

We reached the beautiful mountain town of Samoëns as a storm-induced premature dusk settled over the valley. Our first stop was the cobblestone market-square in the center of the town, where we stocked up on groceries. We also went into a bookstore. I was concerned about carrying extra weight, but I'd finally decided that I needed something to keep me occupied during the long, rainy, tent-bound evenings after I'd finished writing my marathon letters home. I approached the owner and asked her in my best French if she could recommend a novel. She led me to the English-language shelf.

"No," I replied, "I'm looking for something in French." She eyed me skeptically.

"I read a lot better than I speak," I mumbled, my eyes on the floor. "Honest."

She led me to another shelf, this one filled with novels by Stephen King, John Grisham, and Danielle Steele translated into French. "Do you have anything written by a French author?" I asked. "Maybe from this area?"

Her face lit up. "Ah," she said. "I have just the thing." I followed her to an out of the way corner of the shop, where she moved two bookcases and knelt down in front of the bottom shelf of a final case. "Here it is. *Le Grand Crevasse*." On her recommendation I bought the book, and over the next few days as we headed toward Mont Blanc I read it in my sleeping bag – in the dark, with howling winds and freezing rain rattling the sides of the tent. *Le Grand Crevasse* is the story of a climbing guide who falls into a crevasse in the ice on Mont Blanc, spends a week trying to get out, and dies of exposure minutes after he is rescued. I'm nowhere near as impressionable as David, but as he began pestering me about wanting to hike the Tour de Mont Blanc, I couldn't help but get the sense it was a really bad idea. But I'm getting ahead of myself.

It was starting to rain seriously when we reached the campsite and set up our tents. David and I went to a small restaurant next door and had a celebration dinner for me, that day being my 56th birthday. As we got back to the campsite, the rain, which had been torrential up to that point, turned apocalyptic. Holy cow! Combine all the rain we'd had so far, and send it down all at once. From the time lapse between the flashes of light and the thunder peals, I could tell that the lighting was striking nearly on top of us. I fell asleep not convinced that we would survive until morning.

We did survive the night, and in the drizzling morning paid €2.50 ($3.50) to put a load of soggy clothes into the dryer while deciding whether to chance the weather for the 3,500 foot climb up to the Refuge d'Anterne. By the time we finally decided to ignore the weather and walk anyway, it was 11 am. Within minutes, it started raining hard again.

As we left the campground we stopped at a patisserie and bought bread for lunch and a pastry each for a pre-lunch walking snack. As you may have gathered by now, David likes to eat frequently and we came into constant conflict on the subject. At 10 am most mornings he'd start complaining that he was starving and had to have a snack. At 11:30 he'd start whining that it was time for lunch. By 2:00 he'd be ready for his early afternoon snack, and by 5 pm he was ready for his pre-dinner meal. (By the way, he's lean as a whippet. I guess all that sexual energy burns a lot of calories.) I, on the other hand, eat long and hard at breakfast and dinner and could just as well skip lunch. *(Note from David: And whereas I finished the trip looking no different than usual, Dad looked like a centerfold for* Anorexic Mountain Man *magazine.)*

It rained hard for the first 2 hours of the walk. We stopped under the roof of a sheltered fountain just before starting the 5-mile, 1,200-yard climb up to the Refuge d'Anterne. After 3½ more hours – and they were really hard hours – we reached the refuge. We were lucky to get a place to sleep. Apparently the refuge books up months ahead in the summer, but because of the weather they'd been getting some cancellations. In any case, the place was almost full to capacity when we arrived.

The refuge was a ramshackle collection of small buildings. We entered the main building through the eating area, a tiny room crammed with eight six-person eating tables. The whole place was filled with hikers in various stages of partial dress. Half-empty backpacks were everywhere, soggy boots were drying out in front of the small, gas space heater, and clothes were draped from clotheslines strung in front of the windows. Upstairs there was sleeping space, literally in the rafters, for 16 people. Lean-tos with a single toilet and shower were appended to the outside of the building. Another small building about 25 yards away had sleeping space for 29 more people.

We decided to go with the *demi-pension* (half-board) option, which included a bed, dinner and breakfast, and we settled down at one of the tables to dry out, warm up, and wait for the evening meal service to begin. While we were waiting, we struck up a conversation with our tablemates, a French couple and their 14-year-old daughter who were from Annecy, 60 or so miles to the west. They ordered hot mulled wine and gave us some. Then we ordered more and gave them some. It's amazing what three or four glasses of wine will do for your ability to speak in a foreign language.

They assured us (as had everyone else in Switzerland and France) that it almost never rains in that part of the Alps at that time of year. I confessed that it was probably my fault. (A month later I saw in the newspapers that, depending on where and how you measured it, this had been the second or third wettest summer in history in Northern Europe. I really need to start hiring myself out as a rainmaker.)

Refuge d'Anterne

We ate a splendid dinner of soup and cheese fondue. The cook came out and gave us a second helping of the fondue, and we chatted with him about our trek. He went back into the kitchen and came back with an information board he was making. It had the number of days' walk that the refuge is from each end of the GR5, which goes from Amsterdam to Nice, and the Via Alpina Red Route, which goes from Trieste to Monaco. The board was complete except for filling in the numbers of days, and he had been asking likely looking backpackers if they could help him with those final pieces of information. (I guess by that time, with our filthy, torn clothes and my shaggy gray beard, we looked "likely.") He was appreciative when I told him about the Via Alpina website, which I knew had the information he was looking for.

At 9 pm we settled into our beds in the rafters. Although "quiet time" was supposed to start at 10 pm, a half dozen people continued to sit, drink, and carouse in the eating room for at least another hour. Then they came up into the rafters and stumbled around whispering

167

and giggling for another half hour before they settled down. With so many people crammed shoulder-to-shoulder in such a small space, the air was stifling. I decided that in the future I would avoid mountain huts other than when absolutely necessary. That night, though, we were at 7,500 feet, 3½-hours' walk from civilization in one direction and 4-hours' in the other. Outside, the temperature was near freezing, and it was absolutely pouring down rain. If that doesn't classify as being absolutely necessary, it's pretty close.

As we walked away from the refuge in the morning there wasn't a cloud in the sky. The area we were in, which we had seen almost none of the day before because of the clouds and rain, was stunningly beautiful – an isolated mountain valley well above the timber line, with huge cliffs on one side and hills on two of the others.

We walked over one of the sets of hills, past a lake, and up to the Col de Anterne (7,448 ft). As we walked up the last few steps to the col, a panoramic view of Mont Blanc and its surrounding mountains opened suddenly in front of us. Descending over the next 4 hours, that view changed constantly and I didn't take my eyes off it the entire time. Every few steps I would notice significant differences in the vista – what we could see of Mont Blanc massif because of the smaller mountains in front, what we could see of the range of peaks behind, the angle at which the sun reflected off the snowfields and glaciers, the way the clouds obscured and then revealed portions of the massif. Endlessly fascinating and truly breathtaking!

About halfway down, we came to a paragliding launch site. Paragliding, kind of a cross between parachuting and hang-gliding, is a popular Alpine sport, and dozens of paragliders soared back and forth across the valley in front of us as they slowly descended to the city of Passy 2,500 feet below. We considered pitching our tents in the campground next to the launch site, but it was filled with noisy young teenagers, so we pushed on down the hill to the village of Servoz at the bottom of the valley, a few miles from Chamonix and Mont Blanc.

Tour de Mont Blanc

David   July 26th-28th

"I believe in evolution. But I also believe, when I hike the Grand Canyon and see it at sunset, that the hand of God is there also."
– John McCain[18]

First of all, the rain in Samoëns was clearly Dad's fault. That morning as we were breaking camp in Montriond he had made a comment about how lucky we'd been that so far this trip we'd never had to make or break camp in the rain. I stood there dumbfounded, unable to believe that he would actually say such a thing, for that evening and the following morning we had to do both in a torrential downpour. Asshole!

We had just entered a section of the French Alps called, *Les Grands Massifs*, which, for those of you who don't speak French, roughly translates to, "The Big Massives." These mountains happen to be quite large, which is a characteristic that really doesn't distinguish them from the rest of the Alps at all, though they do include Mont Blanc, the highest mountain in Western Europe, at approximately 15,500 feet.

We were not intimidated, though. And by "we" I mean "me." Dad was incredibly intimidated. I had spent the better part of a week trying to talk him into doing the Tour de Mont Blanc with me, and he had resisted from the start, still hung over from our hike from Lenk to Gsteig. Then, in Samoëns he had read a newspaper article about the dozen or so people who die on Mont Blanc every year. He had

---

[18] This is not an endorsement, my friends.

also bought a French novel about a mountain guide who falls into a crevasse and freezes to death. So now he was dead-set against it. Every time I brought it up he would whine like a little girl about how hard it would be, how much walking it was, how he doesn't enjoy those walks, how uncomfortable he is at being that far away from civilization, how dangerous it is, why would we do that to ourselves, and "I'm 56 years old, dammit, what do I have to prove?!" I wanted to do it for the adventure, and the maps made it look like a spectacular walk to boot, and I got really annoyed that he was being such a cry-baby.

We decided to take a rest day and took the train into Chamonix, a touristy but rather charming little city on the base of Le Grand Massif. Among the many errands we ran – grocery shopping, purchasing camping equipment that was lost or needed replacing *(Note from Don: We had to buy a ground cloth to replace the one David left at the Refuge D'Anterne. Hello? David? Is anybody there?)*, and, of course, a huge restaurant lunch – we stopped into the *Maison du Montagne* (the House of the Mountains), which has the answers to all questions Mont Blanc.

We were able to put to rest all of Dad's concerns – the weather would be fantastic, the "difficult" sections are only a problem in the spring when there's snow on the ground, thousands of people hike it every day, and Dad was just being a big blubbering milquetoast.[19]

We made reservations at mountain huts, bought groceries, and headed home where I cooked a fabulous salmon sandwich, which I smothered with most of a bottle of salad dressing. (I'm sure you're sick of hearing the details of what we ate, but I still have fond memories of that sandwich.) Then in the morning we packed up quickly and took the train to St. Gervais, where we caught a bus to Les Contamines-Montjoies, where the portion of the Tour de Mont Blanc we had selected began. From there we climbed 3,000 feet in a couple of hours. There were people everywhere making this ridiculously steep uphill trek: fat people, old people, children,

---

[19] I know ... pretty weak, as far as insults go. But what I had in here originally was far too offensive for the likes of my milquetoasty father.

teenagers. The trail was very wide, and occasionally we'd see an ATV rumbling uphill and over rocks. It all looked like a truck commercial. Every time we saw one I'd make the mental caption: "Professional Driver. Closed Course. Do Not Attempt."

Finally we reached the Croix du Bonhomme (Gentleman's Cross), with the Refuge du Bonhomme 50 yards down the hill. It was a clear day, and outside the hotel was a placard identifying the peaks in all directions and how far away they were. The furthest peak we could see was 52 km (31 miles) away.

As we sat in the dining room waiting for dinner there was a Tower of Babel of languages all around us – French, German, Dutch, Spanish, Italian, various Scandinavian languages, a Slavic language (definitely not Russian, but that's as far as Dad was willing to commit), and English spoken with American, British, Australian, and New Zealand accents. At dinner we sat with two Danish families and their young teenage daughters who were traveling together. The parents were very talkative and the girls spent most of the evening reading – one of them had the latest Harry Potter book, in English. Dad has said that he's never met a Dane who wasn't classy, intelligent, and well educated, and these people were certainly no exception. We talked about everything imaginable, from our trip to U.S. politics to Dad's experiences in Iran. I marveled at how well these people were able to carry on a conversation in English about the long-term impact of the Ayatollah in Iran. I can't even carry on a conversation in English about that.

I stayed up that night to wait for the stars. For the entire trip Dad had been raving about how many billions of stars he could see every time he woke up for his midnight micturation, so I decided it was time for me to witness them for myself. The weather was not going to make it easy, but at this altitude we would probably be above much of the cloud cover. When I noticed the sun going behind the mountain, I headed up the hill to the Croix du Bonhomme to watch the rest of the sunset. The clouds had been pushing past the front door of the Refuge, and the 50-yard climb was enough to rise above them. I watched as the clouds moved through the valley in front of me, squeezed between a narrow pass and headed for the Refuge. To the west the sky was red, fading into blue up above, and to the east the moon was lighting up the clouds like a headlamp in the fog.

Bonhomme Sunset – Ooh, look at the colors![20]

It got very cold, so after a while I decided to go back inside to warm up, watching some people play Scrabble in French – poorly. They chatted with me every now and then and asked if there were any words I didn't understand. There was one I didn't recognize – *anale* – which prompted a round of raucous laughter among the players. At that reaction, I figured it out pretty quickly.

Scrabble is a much easier game in French. Whereas S is just about the only tile you can reliably add to the end of an English word, in French there are a whole host of letters that alter the

---

[20] If we'd printed this book in color it would've cost you $50. We figured it wasn't worth it, for the one picture that didn't translate. Go to www.upsanddownsbook. com to see this picture in all its glory.

conjugation of a verb or the gender of a noun or adjective. For example, there is the aforementioned word, *anale*, which is masculine without the *e* but feminine with it. Verb conjugations end variously with *s*, *t*, *ons*, *ions*, *i*, *e*, *er*, and probably a dozen other combinations of very common letters. But these folks didn't quite grasp the strategy of the game, so I wondered idly if I could beat them.

I read my book in French, and continued to wait and wait for the stars. They never made it out in full force – the moon was too bright – and I had a terrible time sleeping because my toiletry bag had disappeared from the apparently not-so-safe place I'd put it outside our dorm room. (It turned out someone had turned it into the lost and found, so I got it back the next morning.)

The next day would be a long and arduous walk, requiring us to go downhill about 700 feet, uphill about 1,300 feet to the Col de Four, downhill another 3,000 feet, uphill another 2,600 feet, and then downhill some more, before getting to our destination, the Refugi d'Elizabetta across the border in Italy. This was probably the most dangerous hike of the trip for me, not because the trail was difficult but because I spent the entire time looking at the views instead of at the ground underneath me. As we crossed the Col de Four (passing our Danish tablemates in the process), the valley before us continued to open up, and for the next 2 hours we got a completely different view with every 15 steps we took. Off in the distance we could see the pass we were heading toward and knew that the only way to get there was to go all the way down and then all the way up again. We realized at that moment how crazy this whole thing was, that people have to be out of their minds to attempt something like this, and for not the first time I became very emotional and was brought almost to tears at how much of a privilege it was to have the experience.

Frequently on this trip Dad and I had exchanged a conversation that went something like this:

Me: "God, they don't know what they're missing!"

Dad: "Who?"

Me: "Everyone who's not doing this!"

And walking down the soft, broken trail toward the stream that cut the valley in two, was the moment that most epitomized the glory of our journey.

Reader, you truly do not know what you're missing.

Day 2 of the Tour de Mont Blanc turned out to be easier than anticipated. We reached the Col de la Seigne – the border between France and Italy – at about 1:00 in the afternoon, and made tuna sandwiches for lunch. Because of the wind, I took shelter in a tiny hut that was covered head to toe in twenty years worth of graffiti from people marking their accomplishments – crossing the Pyrenees, hiking here from Spain, and so on. I found an empty spot, grabbed a pen, and marked our accomplishment accordingly: "DKF + DRF / TRAVERSÉE LA SUISSE / TRAVERSÉE LE GRAND MASSIF" (Crossed Switzerland, Crossed the Big Mountain). I later realized that I had made a grammatical error that made us women, but hey, you can't win all the time.

We came to the Refugi d'Elizabetta half an hour later. A few days earlier we had called from the Maison du Montagne to try to make reservations in the refugi and had learned that it was booked up. The proprietor had told us that we could pitch our tents outside, but because: (a) it was a good 50 yards up a steep hill from the trail; (b) we'd heard bad things about the refugi from our Danish tablemates the night before; and (c) it was still fairly early and we were feeling good; we decided to press on.

It was obvious we were heading back to civilization. Though we'd seen lots of people through the whole Tour de Mont Blanc, the population suddenly doubled, and there was a gravel road heading directly downhill from the mountain hut and visible all the way through a broad valley. We could see that the road switched back down a steep hill, and then immediately leveled out at the bottom and would be perfectly level for another 2 miles, so we went on with the expectation that we would set up camp once we were inside the valley and the ground was flat.

When we got there, though, it seemed to be a little conspicuous. There was nowhere we could go that was sheltered by trees, and nowhere we wouldn't be seen by the hundreds of people walking up and down the gravel road. Since we weren't entirely sure how legal it was to camp there, we (against my protests and constant complaints) did the entire portion of the walk we'd been expecting to do the next day, eventually finding our way into the outskirts of the municipality of Courmayeur.

We settled into the first campground we came to, where the woman in the office waved her hands constantly as she spoke. Dad, who was concentrating on speaking and understanding Italian, didn't notice, but I couldn't stop laughing on the inside. It's nice to know stereotypes exist for a reason.

A few hundred yards down the road was another campsite with two fancy restaurants, where Dad and I celebrated with a four-course gourmet "Welcome-to-Italy" meal: tagliatelli with porcini mushrooms, gnocchi with cheese sauce, mixed salads, trout almondine, mixed grill, chocolate mousse made with amaretto, and a bottle of excellent Italian red wine. Man, these Italians know how to eat. We ate like that everywhere we went in Italy, constantly astounded at how good the food was, but this meal was far and away the best.

And the Winner Is: The Italian No-Smoking Law

Don   July 29th-31st

While we were waiting for the restaurant to open for dinner, David and I sat outside on the patio for an hour nursing a bottle of wine. The temperature dropped quickly as the sun set behind the cliffs. With the sudden cooling, a strong wind came rushing down the valley from the heights of the pass 5,000 feet above. Nonetheless, we seriously considered staying outside for the entire meal – me because I couldn't face the thought of sitting through a meal in a restaurant full of chain-smoking Italians, and David because he couldn't face the thought of me bitching constantly about sitting through a meal in a restaurant full of chain-smoking Italians.

I had been in Italy on business dozens of times over the previous 20 years, and between 1999 and 2001, I had worked in Turin Monday through Friday nearly every week. My experience was that the Italians would smoke anything that would burn, and they would smoke it without pause. There were few places where smoking was not allowed, and the Italians would ignore the few restrictions that there were (along with stop signs, red lights and no parking signs). As many times as I flew into the Turin airport, I never stopped feeling personally violated by the sight of the machine-gun-toting security guard in the baggage claim area standing underneath the no-smoking sign with a lit cigarette in his mouth.

Eventually, the cold and wind got the better of us, and we reluctantly went inside. To my amazement, there were no-smoking signs in every room. I asked the restaurant owner about it. He said that a national law had come into effect in January 2005, banning smoking in all indoor places unless they have a separate smoking area with continuous floor to ceiling walls and a separate ventilation system. I knew that all those letters of complaint that I had been writing to the Italian prime minister were going to do some good eventually!

On a more somber note, I feel I have to tell you about the critical toilet seat situation in Southern Europe. The farther south you go, the less likely you are to find toilet seats. If you are lucky, there will be two porcelain feet, strategically placed over a hole in the floor. You pull down your pants and underwear, squat, and try to (a) keep your balance and not fall into the hole; and (b) not crap on your clothes. If you are less lucky, the toilet will have been made not to have a raisable seat at all. It will either have a pair of built-in wooden ass-cheek targets – I guess to keep you from sliding into the bowl – or it will have a smooth, broad porcelain rim. In that case you can tell that there was never supposed to be a seat because there are no holes where the seat fittings would have gone.

But at least in both those cases the part where you are supposed to sit is wide enough to support your butt cheeks in relative comfort. If you are unluckiest of all, and unfortunately, this is by far the most common, the toilet was supposed to have a seat, but it has long since broken off and not been replaced. I know all of you North Americans and Northern Europeans will feel serious compassion for the suffering of the French and the Italians and will want to help alleviate this situation. So please consider donating your unwanted but still functional toilet seats to a charity that I will be setting up for this purpose. Watch for the announcements.

The next morning David and I took the bus into Courmayeur. Courmayeur is a bustling skiing and hiking destination and, being situated at the east end of the Mont Blanc tunnel, it is a major stop on the transit links between southern France and northern Italy. The main reason for our trip into town was to find an Internet café to research where we should head next. We had discussed it quite a bit over the previous week and had decided to make a change from the Via Alpina, which would have meant more alpine walking, more alpine mountain huts, and probably lots more rain. Instead, after spending a good part of the morning surfing the Internet in a bar/pizza restaurant, we decided we'd take the train to the coast at

Genoa to do some sightseeing. From there we'd take the train to Riomaggiore, a quaint village perched on the coastal hills about 2 hours east of Genoa. Riomaggiore is in the Cinque Terre (Five Lands) National Park, and is at one end of a famous walking trail running along the cliffs high above the water. At the other end of that trail, we'd walk north into the hills to hook up with the Apennine equivalent of the Appalachian Trail, which we would then follow southeast into the Appenine Mountains in the spine of Italy. The Apennines are much smaller than the big, nasty alpine mountains we'd been hiking through so far. We would also come across lots of small villages, and the terrain, food, culture, and views would be very different from what we'd been experiencing for the previous 5 weeks. Or at least that was the plan that came out of 2 hours of me trolling through mostly Italian-language web sites while David drank beer and wrote e-mails home.

The rest of the day we spent wandering around the town. Whereas in Switzerland nearly everything had been simple and functional and in France everything had been slightly less simple and slightly less functional, now that we were in Italy everything was beautifully designed but not much actually worked. For example, in several places in the town there were computerized information kiosks with attractive, multi-colored displays. But if the computer terminal would do anything at all when we pushed the buttons, either the system would blow up or the links that were supposed to lead to English displays would go to French displays or somewhere else they were not intended to go. Because of my years working in Italy, I knew to expect this, and had warned David that it would happen. Sometimes it can be frustrating, but when you know it's coming and are in the right mood, it's rather comical.

In mid-afternoon I took the bus back up to the campground while David stayed behind and spent most of a $40 phone card having phone sex with Angela. *(Note from David: At this point it was not really phone sex so much as it was a phone massage. This particular phone booth was far too public for phone sex, which would come later on in the trip.)* The road from town up to the campground was steep, winding and narrow, in several places little more than one lane wide. The bus driver, as is common on mountain roads, would honk his horn before going around a turn. This was intended to warn oncoming cars. But it also served to scare the bejeezus out of the bikers that he had come quietly up behind, which he seemed to thoroughly enjoy.

By the time I got to the campground, the afternoon wind was starting to blow down the valley at gale force. I stood in front of my tent and watched in horror as a gust broke the head off one of my tent stakes. This allowed the next gust to lift the tent off the trekking pole that I was using as a tent pole and push the fabric down on the pole, ripping a hole through the top of the tent. I spent the next hour cutting small squares from a black plastic trash bag that I carry in my emergency kit and trying to glue them onto the hole. Each time I thought I had a patch that would hold and tested the edge with my finger, it would peel off and I had to start over. Eventually David showed up from Courmayeur, and with his help we managed to devise something that succeeded in keeping the rain out for the next 3 weeks. Thank goodness for the emergency repair supplies I'd been carrying around for the last 6 weeks.

Speaking of emergency supplies, that topic had been a bone of contention between David and me from the beginning of the trip. I tend to be a bit of a worrier about walking in the mountains and want to be prepared to deal with most foreseeable problems. Consequently, in addition to the normal shelter, sleeping and cooking gear and clothes, I was carrying a basic first aid and medicine kit (including plenty of high-tech blister treatment pads and drugs to fit every occasion), chlorine water-purification drops, a pocket knife, waterproof matches, 2 cigarette lighters, a candle, a small GPS, a magnetic compass (in case the GPS doesn't work), spare batteries (for the ultra-violet water-purifier, the headlamps and the GPS), extra toilet paper, a foil hypothermia-prevention blanket, 2 black plastic trashbin liners, a thin waterproof ground-cloth/poncho, the cell phone we picked up in Altdorf (which had a charger that weighed about a pound) and a writing pad and pen. All that stuff weighed more than I was happy carrying, and I complained about it often. Several times David insisted that I was carrying a lot of things we didn't need, so we'd lay it all out on the ground and go through the items one by one. And one by one, I'd refuse to discard anything, and pack it all back up again. Over the course of the trip we used everything except the foil hypothermia blanket, a few of the bandages, and a few of the medicine tablets. Many of them we needed only once or twice, but on those occasions we were certainly glad to have them. *(Note from David: A few? A few?! We used hardly any of the three dozen types of pills he brought – I think Angela might have used an aspirin once – nor did we use the compass, the sewing kit, the "signaling mirror," or any of the other "emergency items" Dad insisted we carry but has since forgotten we didn't use.) (Riposte from Don: David is conveniently forgetting about the time he needed the Alka-Seltzer for an upset stomach that he claimed bordered on being fatal. I used the sewing kit to repair an article of clothing. The "dozens of types of pills" he refers to were about 6 tablets each of aspirin, ibuprofen, Tylenol, anti-diarrhea tablets, and a cold remedy / anti-histamine that I'd put into a small, single container. OK, so we didn't use the signaling mirror, the whistle or the magnetic compass. That's kind of the point of emergency supplies. You carry them in case of emergencies, and you hope you aren't going to need every one of them. Next time David goes trekking for 2 months – provided he goes without me – his full complement of emergency gear can be the plastic figure of Ronald McDonald from a Happy Meal.)*

When David got back from Courmayeur we ate a very uncomfortable meal with the wind growing stronger by the minute and blowing our food, plates and silverware away as we tried to hold them down. We settled into our tents for the night, with me hoping that the top-puncturing episode wouldn't be repeated and that my make-shift patch would hold.

The gale got stronger and stronger. Every few seconds the inside of tent would puff out like a sail; then the wind would shift suddenly and the material would come crashing down with a pop. I was absolutely convinced that my flimsy, ultra-light shelter would rip itself apart. As the tent inflated and deflated like a gigantic bellows for the next 3 hours, I alternated between holding down the bottom edges to keep it from flying away and bracing my hands against the side walls to keep it from driving itself down over the tent pole.

Around 11 pm, I went out and lowered the top and sides of the tent to provide less wind resistance. This helped for a while, but the wind continued to grow. Around midnight, I heard a tremendous commotion from the side where David had pitched his tent. I looked out and saw a big pile of canvas and a struggling body; the wind had pulled out one of the stakes and his tent had collapsed around him. Fortunately, the poles had just fallen over rather than piercing the top of the tent. At that point I told him that it was a bad idea for him to re-erect the tent and that I was going to pull mine down as well before the gale destroyed it completely.

The previous night, anticipating that something like this might happen, I had scoped out the campground for likely shelter and had decided that the dish-washing hut would fit the bill. So we battened down the tents flat on the ground with water bottles and other water-proof gear as well as we could to keep our other gear protected, and moved into the dish-washing hut with our sleeping bags and pads. For the next several hours, the metal roof of the hut banged like mad, and I was sure that it was going to blow off. Eventually, I fell into a fitful sleep. When I awakened around 5 am I noticed that the wind had died and it was starting to rain. I went out and set up my tent and then went back to wake up David to get him to do the same. We then moved into our tents and slept until about 8:30, when we were awakened by sound of one of the maintenance men using a leafblower. I don't think there's any way to express the irony we felt in that moment when, after spending the entire night trying to keep from being blown into the next dimension, we rolled over and saw the leaves floating past our tents on a beautiful, calm, sunny morning. Amazing that nature can be so violent one moment and so beneficent the next.

The bus for Courmayeur was leaving in 15 minutes, and if we missed it we would have to wait 90 minutes for the next one. It usually took us more than an hour to break camp, but by this time we were getting pretty good at it, and we rushed to the road just as the bus pulled up. A few hundred yards down the road, the bus stopped, and our Danish tablemates from Refuge du Bonhomme trouped on. We had a joyful reunion; it's amazing how quickly you can bond with people in the mountains. In Courmayeur fifteen minutes later we caught another bus that went directly to the Aosta train station, a 70-minute, 30-mile drive away. Ten minutes after that we were on a third bus for the 2-hour, 90-mile bus ride to Turin.

While waiting the 2½ hours in Turin for the next train that was leaving for Genoa, we found a nice, small restaurant, ate ourselves silly, and then took a lightning walking tour of the old city. My

Italian was coming back quickly, and from my days of working in Turin on several projects for Fiat, I knew the city fairly well. The far northwest of Italy was occupied by the Counts of Savoy for 800 years, and much of the culture and architecture has been heavily influenced by them. Turin was made the capital of the Duchy of Savoy in the middle of the 16th century, and it was the capital of the newly proclaimed United Italy from 1861 to 1864. So while most of Turin is characterized by the drab, industrial legacy of being Fiat's headquarters for the last hundred years, the downtown area has many lovely palaces and majestic government buildings.

The big shock was that it was 94°F (34°C) and 80% humidity. What a change after 6 weeks in the mountains, much of it cold and rainy, and the rest of it cool and pleasant.

At 4 pm we caught the Intercity train for the 110-mile, 2-hour trip to Genoa. In Italian train-speak, Intercity means slightly more expensive, fewer stops, and all first class compartments. I say "slightly more expensive." The whole trip that day – three buses and a train, encompassing 225 miles and 5 hours and 15 minutes of travel time – cost €25.70 per person (~$36). In Switzerland, the 1-hour train ride from Interlaken to Zurich costs CHF 65, which is €40.

Sitting in the air-conditioned first-class train compartment that afternoon was an incredible luxury, and we dreaded reaching Genoa and having to hoist our backpacks and start wandering the streets in the blazing sun in search of accommodation. But all too soon we were walking from the Genoa train station to the tourist information office in the old section of the town. We tried several hotels before we found the 1-star Hotel Major in an area of narrow alleys with cobblestone streets. I was thoroughly wilted after a day in 90+° heat, so I stayed in the hotel to take a shower and wash my clothes, while David went out to explore the town.

Mandi and Paolo 4EVER!

David   **July 30th-August 2nd**

It had been my idea to spend some time in Genoa, though Lord knows why I wanted to. I suppose I was inspired by Shakespeare's reference to the city in *The Merchant of Venice*, and for some reason I thought it would be a fun place to hang out. In the end, it was a fairly typical Italian city – by which I mean there are hundreds of old churches and every single thing without exception is covered in graffiti.

Dad, having worked in Italy for several years, was prepared for this, but I was shocked and appalled. Everywhere we turned we'd see 12th century monuments with someone's initials scrawled across them, or a garden with "YOU SAY IT BEST WHEN YOU SAY NOTHING AT ALL" spray-painted on the rock paths between the flower beds, or a 9th century church with the words, "MANDI + PAULO 4EVER" decorating the façade. It was truly disgusting. Later on, in Cinque Terre, we saw that even the cacti had graffiti on them. I wondered if a guy ever showed something like that to his girlfriend only to have her react by saying, "I can't believe you would deface public property like that! I'm leaving you!" to which her boyfriend would no doubt reply, "But it says Mandi and Paulo *4EVER!*"

In spite of the way the citizens had chosen to decorate it, we had a pleasant enough time wandering through the city. We walked for probably as much as 8 miles up and down narrow cobblestone streets, many of which are no more than 7 feet wide and 100 feet long. The buildings were mostly 4-5 stories high and had stores on the ground floor and residences above, creating a canyon-like effect. At the end of each block you come to a crossroads and there will be a tiny piazza, usually with a medieval church. Some of the bigger streets are lined with Renaissance palaces from the 16th and 17th centuries, a number of which have been turned into museums or are now used as official buildings.

Cactal Graffiti

We had reached the city right in the middle of a "tall ships festival," so we walked through the harbor, which was lined with hundreds of hideously decorated and painfully impractical ships sporting names like "The Amerigo Vespucci" and "The Dutch Whaler." Several of these were available for public exploration, and we got to experience the joy of the world's largest brigantine-rigged ship.[21] To us it looked just like a regular ship, but with more hype. But hey, we had a good time going through it anyway.

And of course we engaged in our new favorite pastime, eating Italian food.

After a day and a half we'd had more than enough of Genoa, and were ready to leave. We got our passports back from the hotel (I was a little disturbed at having to surrender them when we checked in, but apparently that's common practice in Italy), and went to the train station. Dad stood in line at the ticket counter while I stood in line at one of the automated machines, while the time ticked away. At 9:16 – four minutes before our train was scheduled to leave – I got to the front of my line and began navigating my way through the automated ticket machine, which, like everything else in Italy, is beautiful to look at but doesn't really work. After taking 2 minutes to get to the payment screen, it didn't like my debit card, but rather than having a "select alternate payment" option we had the choice between inserting a valid debit card (which apparently I didn't have) or canceling out of the whole thing and starting all over again. On the verge of panic, I managed to extract two tickets with 30 seconds to spare, Dad abandoned his place in the ticket counter queue, and we sprinted to the platform. We got there at exactly 9:20... and then waited 18 minutes for the train to arrive. Weren't we lucky that the scheduled departure times for Italian trains bear absolutely no relation to reality?

In the chaos of buying our tickets we'd accidentally gotten first class seats, and found ourselves sitting next to an Australian couple, two of the most beautiful people on the planet. Sarah was a flight attendant for Virgin Blue, which has a reputation for having

---

[21] A brigantine is a ship with exactly two masts, at least one of which is square-rigged. A square rig is an arrangement in which the primary driving sails are carried on horizontal spars, which are perpendicular to the keel and masts. A spar is any round pole used on a ship. The keel is ... ah, screw it.

gorgeous flight attendants. She was tall, had stunning facial features, and to say she had an hourglass figure is to give too much credit to hourglasses.

Jordan, her husband, had just graduated from university with degrees in business and law, which sparked a rather heated debate between him and Dad on the necessity of lawyers and/or the justifiable animosity toward them in society. Dad often talks about having spent his entire business career battling "those unethical bastards," which gives you a pretty good idea of how he feels on the subject. Jordan stood up for his kind, arguing that everybody loves to hate lawyers, but where would we be without them? To Dad, that's like asking where we would be without pubic lice (which, to be fair, are remarkably similar parasites in a number of ways). In neither case would there be too many downsides to complete extinction, and any downsides that did exist we could probably live with.

For a while, I thought Dad and Jordan were going to come to blows, but Dad finally realized that it would be impossible to win an argument with a 23-year-old pre-law graduate, and ended the conversation by saying magnanimously, "I'm sure you're going to be the exception." Did I hear a hint of irony in his voice?

Jordan and Sarah were going to the same place we were – Riomaggiore, part of the Cinque Terre National Park, where the total population is about 6,000 locals and, during the summer at least, 600,000 tourists. We hadn't yet figured out the reason why we (I) had been so depressed on the shores of Lac Léman, and in our search for something new and exciting we thought coming here was the solution.

It wasn't.

Don't get me wrong. Riomaggiore is a nice enough place. If you like beaches and quaint little towns with dozens of restaurants and souvenir shops where the locals approach you in English before trying the local language, then you'd no doubt have an extraordinary time there. If you happen to be an Italian male looking to pick up American women, then this is definitely the place for you. It's just that we realized there, as we had a couple of weeks earlier on Lac

Léman and as we would again in Monterosso the next day, that beaches weren't our thing.

There were dozens of agencies that rented rooms, and we arbitrarily picked one. The agent led us down the main street and then unexpectedly cut off into an alleyway we hadn't even noticed on our first pass through the town. We followed him up stairs, down stairs, around corners, twisting and turning through a narrow alley no more than 3 feet wide. It took us about 3 minutes of this to get to our building. All the while we developed a growing sense of dread that there was no way on earth we'd be able to find our way out of there, much less back.

But our room had a perfect, unobstructed view of the Mediterranean, so we gladly agreed to take it, and quickly found our way around the alleys with no trouble at all. We purchased fruit and yogurt for lunch and returned to find the maid preparing our room for us.

I wanted to lie down because I'd been sick for the past day. I'm not sure if it was something in particular I ate or just the accumulation of all the rich foods we'd been eating over the past few days, but on our second night in Genoa I hadn't been interested in eating dinner. That's a sure sign I'm sick, since I'm usually interested in eating at least five times a day. But I'd eaten anyway and then thrown up in the middle of the night. In the morning I'd drunk some tea and forced myself to eat a banana. Although I was feeling a little better now, I still wanted to lie down.

Our maid, however, had other plans. As Dad and I stood in the room talking about our plans for lunch, dinner, and the next day, she grew increasingly agitated and finally said (in Italian), "This is ridiculous! How am I supposed to work like this?" We stood stunned and wondering what to do until she told us to go away and come back in twenty minutes.

We spent the rest of the morning sitting on a rock next to the harbor, flipping through the pages of an Italian edition of *Maxim* which we'd found lying on a rowboat until we got up the courage to return to the room. Then we ate lunch and napped for about 4 hours. We awoke in time to order dinner from the infectiously bubbly owner of a take-out only fast food restaurant, and then stood at the window of our apartment watching the sun set over a peninsula in the distance and listening to the waves lap against the rocks.

'... and she made them wander in the desert 40 years ...'

The following morning we walked on the shore trail through the national park, which ran the length of the Cinque Terre cliffs northwest from Riomaggiore to Monterosso.   We encountered hundreds of people along the way - Americans, Brits, Aussies, Scandinavians, Germans, Italians, French, Dutch, and so on, to the point where we started greeting people by saying, "Buon giorno, hello, grüezi, guten Tag, bonjour," just to make sure we had all the bases covered. There were thousands of steps up and down in the blazing heat along the rocky shoreline, and we were sure that most people had no idea what they were getting themselves into when they thought, "Hey, let's take a stroll through the national park."

I was feeling better by now, having eaten voraciously that morning and snacked at a takeout place in Corniglia, the middle of the five towns in Cinque Terre. Even with the stop, we finished the hike in 3 hours, rather than the five suggested by the park service. Yes! We are men! Strong and masculine!

Monterosso is a larger, busier version of Riomaggiore – at 1,730 locals it is the most populous of the five towns, stretches a mile or more wide, and the beaches have sand rather than exclusively rocks like the shores of Riomaggiore. Instead of dozens of restaurants and souvenir shops there were hundreds of them. There was a larger percentage of Italians there than in Riomaggiore, but that's not saying much – Des Moines, Iowa probably has a higher percentage of Italians than Riomaggiore does.

Finally, we'd had enough and decided it was time to get back into the hills. This was when the real adventure started.

Hiking Hell and Camping Hell

Don   **August 2ⁿᵈ-4ᵗʰ**

Italy is famous for being a very federalist state, which is to say it's very much geared around local culture. Whereas Swiss towns are very similar from one to the next, in Italy when you go from one city to another the people have very different attitudes and lifestyles. Nowhere does this phenomenon manifest itself more than in the Italian tourist information offices.

Starting in Courmayeur, David and I had been trying to find more information on our next trail, the Grande Escursione Apennenica (GEA). We'd gone into tourist information offices and bookstores and had absolutely no success. In Courmayeur they'd never heard of it, which is fair enough since it was still several hundred miles away. We asked in Genoa and received a similar reaction. We really started getting nervous when we asked in Riomaggiore and Monterosso, and they knew nothing about the GEA, which at that point should have been only about 3-days' walk away.

So the afternoon before we were scheduled to leave Monterosso we went into an Internet café. While David composed amusing e-mails to friends back in the States, I surfed the net looking for some clue as to how to start. The best I could find was that the Parco Nazionale Delle Tosco Emiliana, which was where the GEA begins, was somewhere between the towns of Pontremoli and Borgo Val di Taro. Rather than starting to hike 30 miles in a vaguely northeasterly direction, we decided it would be best to take the train to Pontremoli and ask there. The tourist information office in Pontremoli was sure to know all about the trail. And there were certain to be hiking and camping stores to equip the people who came flocking to the park from all over Europe … . Weren't there?

The trail would be mostly over 3,000 feet in altitude and far away from any significant centers of population. After 4 days in the heat, crowding and noise of the coast and the cities, we were looking forward to the cool, isolation and quiet again.

We found Pontremoli's tourist office in the town hall just off the central square. I told the young clerk what we were looking for. "Signorina, cerchiamo il Parco Nazionale Delle Tosco Emiliana. Sa come andiamo qua?" ("Miss, we're looking for the Tosco Emiliana National Park. Do you know how we get there?") She looked at me with a puzzled expression.

"Do you mean the Park of Cinque Terre?" Right then I had a feeling we were in trouble.

"No," I replied. "The Tosco Emiliana National Park. It's right up there," I said uncertainly, pointing toward the eastern wall of the office.

Whereas everyone else we had asked had simply replied, "Not my territory, not my business," this young lady was determined to help. She went over to her Internet terminal and Googled "Parco Nationale Delle Tosco Emiliana." My feeling that we were in trouble blossomed into complete certainty. I didn't have the heart to stop her, and for the next half hour David and I stood and watched her look at all the same sites that I'd been looking at and getting minimal information from for the past 4 days. I politely took the pages that she printed out, as well as half a dozen heavy, colorful, but useless brochures that she proudly bestowed on us. (Twenty minutes later and several hundred yards away, where I was sure she wouldn't come across them, I discarded the whole pile in a trash bin.)

"What about camping stores?" I asked her.

"Oh, no, there are no camping stores in Pontremoli. Maybe in La Spezia [25 miles to the south] or Parma [35 miles to the north]."

We left the information office and found a bookstore where we spent 20 minutes looking through topographical maps, most of which looked as though they'd been printed off on someone's dot matrix printer and then photocopied three times. In the end we found a map that showed the road and trails leading east from Pontremoli toward a large green area that we assumed must be the national park.

Next, we went to stock up on groceries. The stores in Switzerland, no matter how small, always had powdered milk, instant mashed potatoes (gag!), muesli, and lots of other lightweight, easy-to-prepare foods; the stores in France usually had at least something we could carry. In contrast, the stores we had seen in Italy so far, even in the larger towns, seemed to have only heavy, bulky foods that would take lots of preparation. That was certainly the case in the tiny stores in Pontremoli. The prospect of spending the next 4 days having to boil pasta for 20 minutes and then pour over it spaghetti sauce from liter glass jars that we'd have to carry on our backs was not a particularly appealing one.

We asked about powdered milk and were directed to a pharmacy. I suspected that there was a communication problem there. Sure enough, in the pharmacy they offered us baby formula – which we declined. In the end we did the best we could, but it was not nearly as light, of as much variety, or as easy to prepare as what we had been using for the past 6 weeks.

After purchasing the groceries, David and I went into a small trattoria for a "last meal" and had the slowest service on the planet – it took about 2 hours and 15 minutes to be served two courses. I was already stressed out and annoyed when we went into the restaurant, but I was downright pissed by the time we were finished. There were signs all over the place saying that the place took credit cards, but when I offered my card our waitress told me that she could accept only cash.

"But all those signs say that the restaurant takes credit cards," I said.

"The restaurant takes credit cards, but I don't," she replied.

"Then get someone who does," I said.

"They're not here," she said.

"What if I don't have cash," I asked.

She shrugged her shoulders. I considered wrestling her to the floor and beating her into submission, but I realized that probably wasn't a great idea, and after bitching at her for a few more minutes I paid – in cash.

At that point David and I were starting to suspect that somebody upstairs didn't like what we were doing. But we hoisted our backpacks and started heading up the hill into the mountains. As we walked, we noticed that a very large percentage of the houses had security fences around them. Most had dogs as well. At one house, the fence was topped with barbed wire and there was a sign saying that any trespassing would be met with an immediate armed response. It may just be a cultural thing, but I suppose the theft problem is such that these kinds of measures are required.

After about 45-minute walk, we reached Ceretoli, the village where the map said the first footpath was to begin. The path wasn't where the map said it would be. We spent about a half-hour looking all over the village and speaking to the locals, who assured us that there was no footpath in Ceretoli. Eventually, David located a path that headed off 180° in the wrong direction. Better a path in the wrong direction than no path at all, we decided. Several hundred yards outside of the village the path turned and headed in the direction we wanted to go and displayed a sign confirming it was, indeed, the one we were looking for.

After a third of a mile, however, it became completely overgrown with nettles and briars and was absolutely impassable. We detoured through a neighboring olive grove until we saw that the trail had cleared, and we joined it for about another half a mile to where it again became impassable.

This time, we had no choice but to backtrack to a point where we could take a long driveway up the hill to a gravel road. We followed the gravel road, which we located on the map, for about 3 miles. At that point, the map showed that another gravel road would cross the one we were on, and if we turned left and headed up the mountain we would rejoin the footpath. Well, there was a road leading in from the right, but nothing going to the left. We walked ahead another several miles and came to a tiny hamlet with 3 houses and a sign giving its name. But the map showed that the hamlet with that name was supposed to be several miles further. We pressed on and, sure enough, after several miles we came to another village with a sign identifying it as the one which the map said should have been the one we had come to half an hour before.

In the meantime, an old farmer with a long face and a prominent nose and chin came out of a side trail and asked if he could help us. He looked at our map, turned it upside down, looked at a corner of the map 10 miles from where we were, and confirmed that we were hopelessly lost. But if we would continue ahead on the gravel road we were walking on, we would eventually get back to civilization.

By this time it was nearly 6 pm, and David and I were hot, sweaty, frustrated, and getting tired. As near as we could figure, we were at least 2-hour walk from the boundary of the park. And that would be if everything suddenly started to go perfectly. Fat chance! All around us was dense scrub; we hadn't seen anything remotely campable since we had left Pontremoli.

Finally we came to a tiny village with a bus stop. "Ah, screw it," we both decided simultaneously. "Let's get the hell off this mountain." But when we looked at the schedule we discovered that the bus came through twice a day – at 8:25 am and at 8:50 am, which wasn't particularly helpful to us at that moment. The good news, though, was that we learned from the bus stop sign the name of the village we were in … . Maybe.

We headed downhill at the first opportunity. On the way, David, whose sore, aching feet were making him delirious, started fantasizing about alternate ways to descend. I was a bit delirious myself, but I recall something about gathering dried leaves and sliding down the road on our butts. There was also something about tying sticks to our feet and using them as skis. None of his suggestions were entirely practical.

It looked as though we would have another 90-minute walk to civilization, but a half hour later, a man drove a car out of a field near us and headed down the hill. I put out my hand to flag him down and, mercifully, he stopped. I guess we looked pretty miserable, because he drove us to the nearest train station, Scorcetoli, a whistle-stop we had passed on the way to Pontremoli early that morning.

The last train of the day came through Scorcetoli 15 minutes later. We took it 20 minutes north to Borgo Val di Taro, where we got off and found a campground. I boiled up some pasta and dumped a jar of sauce over it while David had a meltdown. He sat there with his head in his hands, whimpering that he wanted to go back to Switzerland, where trails and maps and stores and tourist information offices were as they should be.

David's spirits improved quickly, though. The air was beautifully cool that night, which was a pleasure after the heat of the last 4 days. When we got up the next morning we walked to the center of Borgo and managed to find a reasonable-sized supermarket. It even had peanut butter in a plastic jar. (Ever since we had left Switzerland, we had found only glass which, on weight considerations, we had refused to buy.) Still no powdered milk, though. We bought a big hunk of watermelon, and had a breakfast orgy. (Picture the eating scene from the movie *Tom Jones,* except with two men and no sex afterward.)

By noon we were back at the Borgo station waiting for the train – any train – north. David went to the restaurant next door and came back elbows deep in a döner kebab. A few minutes later, he went back and returned with an ice cream cone. He was about to go back for another döner kebab, but I suggested he wait a while. If it seems that we were getting obsessed with food, that's pretty accurate.

Eventually we caught a (late) train to Parma. The (late) connecting train for Milan, had signs all over it saying "Air-conditioned train, do not open windows except in case of emergency." The air-conditioning was not working and it was easily 120°F (47°C) in there. We, and everyone else on the train, considered that an emergency and opened the windows. We arrived in Milan at 4:40 pm and quickly checked the departure schedule to see when the next train was heading north to Lugano. It was scheduled for 5:30. The machines in the ticket office all said they were for Italian destinations only, so I joined a line of 100 people waiting in the two lines marked "International Destinations." Twenty minutes later, not one person had moved from either line. Fortunately, David had meanwhile been wandering around the terminal and found a ticket machine (nowhere near the ticketing hall) that sold international tickets. Otherwise, I'd still be waiting in that line. The tickets were €31 each – as much as we'd spent on the previous 3-days' transportation combined – and no doubt 90% of that cost was for the 15 minutes that the train would travel from the Swiss border to Lugano.

On the train to Lugano, which was all reserved seats and nearly full, we sat next to a young lady with an American accent who struck up a conversation with us. She had been born in Panama of an Italian mother and an American father, and now lived in Turin. She was incredibly talkative and had strong, loud, mostly negative opinions about most things Italian: the lack of security at airports, incompetent bureaucracy, and of course, loud people with negative opinions . I kept sneaking peeks around the carriage to see if anyone was listening and understanding, and if we were about to get our heads bashed in.

We arrived in Lugano at 6:30, and David found a hotel information office that had a brochure of campgrounds in Ticino (the canton in which Lugano is located). The nearby town of Agno is on the end of Lake Lugano and has 4 campgrounds, but the hotel office thought that on a Saturday night in August they might all be booked up. I got out my cell phone and called one of the campgrounds. To our surprise and delight, it had room.

We hopped on a local commuter train, and 20 minutes later walked into camping hell! The place had potential – it was located right on the shore of the lake, and had beautiful views of the hills all around. Somehow, though, it had gotten a reputation as a young people's paradise. And now I understood why they had room. The place had apparently resolved not to turn anybody away. **EVER!** There were easily three times as many tents on the site as could legitimately be placed on it. They were squeezed in every way imaginable, and the occupants of easily half of them were playing some kind of loud obnoxious music. Every minute or so, we'd be overwhelmed by smoke, sometimes cigarette smoke, but just as often marijuana smoke. Unfortunately, by the time we realized just how terrible the place was, we'd already set up our tents and unpacked. I guess our brains were numb from the heat and exhaustion of the previous 3 days. After cooking dinner we took a walk by several of the other campsites in Agno – quiet, organized, legitimate sites – and we resolved to switch as soon as we could the next morning. Back in camping hell, the music and clouds of marijuana smoke continued well into the night.

South to North Across Switzerland

Trans-Swiss Trail · · · · · · · ·

Jakobspilger Route ▬▬▬

National Boundaries · · · · · · · ·

The $150,000 Free Lunch

David   August 5th-6th

Sympathetic misery is a bitch. I'm not sure if this is just me, but whenever I play someone a song that I really like or show them a movie that I really love or a standup comedy routine I find really funny – I find myself constantly looking over at the person to see if they're enjoying it as much as I am. If they aren't, I inevitably become uncomfortable, just waiting for the thing to be over so the misery can end.

It's a similar phenomenon, of course, when you're with someone you know is unhappy about something but there's not much you can do about it. In other circumstances, I would have enjoyed being at this camping site. It had the flair of something you'd see at Burning Man[22]. It was one massive party, with four different kinds of music blasting within hearing distance and four different kinds of marijuana being smoked within smelling distance. If we had been seeking a social atmosphere of teens and twenty-somethings, this would have been it.

But this wasn't what we were seeking, and even if I could have made the best of it, Dad's misery was infectious. Though we returned to the campsite well after the 10 pm quiet time, people were still playing games at tents that were touching ours, they were playing music from their stereos at an audible volume, and through the night drunk people kept returning sobro vocce from the nearby nightclub. I lay awake well past 2 am, worried about how unhappy Dad surely was.

---

[22] Or, if you're not cool enough to know what Burning Man is, think Woodstock.

I spent some time staring at the stars that night. Even though we were on the lake and it was too hazy to see too many, I've always enjoyed looking at the sky and figuring out what I'd name the constellations, since I can see the groupings but have no idea what they're actually called. I thought about naming a star after Angela – something that's remarkably easy to do. There are so many billions of stars out there, for $50 you can register one, and you get a little packet with the name of the star, where it is in the sky, and a pamphlet saying, "Congratulations. Now all you have to do to actually see your star is look through the ultra-high-magnification telescope at the top of Mount Kilimanjaro! Tours cost $10,000 and include airfare, 2-nights' hotel stay, and a romantic meal at our Kilimanjaro Planetarium."

I made that last part up, though I've often wondered what lengths are required to actually see your star in the sky. Perhaps it's as simple as spending the night on a farm in the middle of Nowhere, West Texas, or at the top of one of Colorado's 14,000-footers. Anyway, the idea's never appealed to me before, but I began thinking about how much fun it would be to have a star named *Spargel Gemüse* (asparagus vegetable), the pet name Angela and I had somehow managed to pick up for each other during this trip.

In the morning we woke up early and, while it was tempting to make as much noise as humanly possible, we broke camp in silence and set out to find another campsite. We'd found La Palma (the campsite we'd just stayed in) in a brochure I'd gotten at the "Hotel Information" office at the Lugano train station, and called it first because it was the cheapest one listed. We soon found out that the prices listed in the brochure had little or nothing to do with the actual prices we'd pay. This place had turned out to be much more expensive than listed, and when we went to the next place, they quoted us a price of 54 francs, more than we'd paid in any of our Massenlagers. The price list featured higher fees for premium spots than the less desirable ones, and they wanted to charge us an additional 10 francs for having two tents instead of one, even though they were both going onto one plot. It was a common practice to charge extra for an extra person, who would be using extra facilities, hot water, and so on, but by now we'd gotten used to everyone giving us a break because our tents were so small. We refused the extra expense and went to the next place, which was supposed to be the most expensive of the four in Agno, but turned out to be only 40 francs per night for plots that were twice as big and infinitely more private.

We picked a nice spot in the shade and spent the day relaxing and vegging out – wading on the imported-sand beach, swimming in the lake yards from our campsite, and doing the perennial clothes wash. That afternoon I went to the post office to use the public phone to try to call Angela. Throughout France and Italy I'd been using Startec, a phone service that Dad has, where we'd dial a toll-free number first and the charges go to his home phone bill. But when I got to the Swisscom phone and tried dialing the 800 number for Startec, I got a message in Italian which I didn't understand, but could only assume meant I couldn't dial that number. After failing several times, I resolved to contact Swisscom to find out more information. I called their 0800 number, navigated their system in French, and eventually got a message that they're open Monday to Friday from 7 am to 10 pm and Saturday from … . I stopped paying attention.

I wandered toward town and soon found another payphone and got the same response. I wandered further and further, desperate to find one, before eventually finding a 4-star hotel, which had several courtesy phones I could use. It took a few tries but I ultimately succeeded and had Angela on the other end of the line.

I went off for fifteen minutes about how frustrated I was. Every time we thought we were going to do something, it didn't work out, and we spent time on beaches in touristy areas, and it was hot and I was lethargic the whole time. I bitched about how Dad was reluctant to go on any crazy adventures and didn't want to walk much anymore. At the end of it all, I was just tired and sad and wanted to go home.

Of course, leaving early was not an option. Before we left, Dad's mother had told him how ridiculous an idea this trip was, and she said to him, "I bet you leave early."

Dad's response had been, "I'll take that bet. Ten thousand dollars?" Of course, no money exchanged hands, but even so we weren't about to give her the satisfaction.

That didn't change the fact that I wanted very much to go home. I was glad to have Angela there to listen to me get everything off my chest. This was the hump – one that Dad had gone through 3 weeks earlier when we walked from Lenk to Lauenen to Gsteig, and I knew it would be a critical and inevitable part of the trip for me, too. Just saying all these things, a tremendous weight came off my shoulders and I was free to look to the future.

Indeed, that was the last of the depression that came during the trip. Though there would be a few more moments of mental anguish, I wouldn't be depressed again until several weeks after I returned home to an empty bank account, a freelance writing business that was in shambles, and of course, no reason to walk 8 miles a day.

Dad and I came back to the hotel later that evening to use the Internet terminal there, and we discovered that we were only 3 miles away from TASIS Lugano, the mother campus of the high school I'd attended in England. We decided we'd spend the next day looking for it and then walk into downtown Lugano before starting the next part of our trip – walking north along the Trans-Swiss Trail to Zurich.

The TASIS Lugano campus is gorgeous. It's built in the town of Montagnola on the hill overlooking Lake Lugano, and looks like an Italian villa, the kind of place you'd imagine an 18th century aristocrat living with his eight children and 200 servants. Some of the dorm rooms have balconies, and walking from one building to another requires climbing a series of cobblestone steps that feature a magnificent view of the lake and the mountains beyond it. Walking through that campus, I came to the realization that these places don't exist for the students, they exist for the parents. Quality of education aside, who wouldn't want their kid going to school in a 12th century village (the TASIS England campus) or an Italian villa?

After a few joyful reunions with people we couldn't possibly have expected to see (the granddaughter of the school's founder, who graduated one year ahead of me at TASIS England and was now working in the administration here; as well as the former headmaster of the TASIS England campus, who was coming out of retirement to celebrate his very first day as the Interim Headmaster in Lugano), we ate lunch for free in the cafeteria *(Note from Don: To think that the company I worked for only paid $25,000 a year for 6 years for that free lunch!)* and then walked back down the hill, through the woods, and into downtown Lugano.

My grandparents had visited Lugano thirty years ago. Of all the places they vacationed in their lives – and they traveled all over the world – this was their favorite. I could see why – though a significant portion of its jobs must be attributable to tourism, it's very unassuming in that regard. Not unlike downtown New York, you know that tourists exist, but their presence is drowned out by the locals who work in the banks or the municipal buildings; by the students at the university; by the suburb-dwellers who come from the hills on the weekend to do their shopping or eat gelato at the cafés; and by the growing number of celebrities and other wealthy people who are using the "Monte Carlo of Switzerland" as their summer home.

Because of its location and its cosmopolitan atmosphere – Italian, French, and English are all readily spoken and German isn't far behind – global businesses are flocking to Lugano as a headquarters location for their European divisions. When TASIS was born, its founders never expected it to be anything but a boarding school, but now they have over 100 day students from locally resident expatriate families from all over the world.

We went to several bookstores in Lugano to find a map for the next part of our route. We'd been spoiled by using Tomas's maps for free and by the reasonable prices of the maps in France. In Lugano we were horrified at the prospect of paying 24 francs for a map that we would walk through in a day and a half. Ultimately we decided we'd rather get lost. I also searched for a book to replace *Around the World in 80 Days*, which I'd bought in Montreux but had now finished, but everything in English was astronomically priced; a 150-page paperback also cost 24 francs. I ended up paying CHF 25.50 for a 250-page Graham Greene novel, which I started reading later that night. It was physically painful shelling out that kind of money for a thin paperback, but having something to read makes a huge difference when you're bored at night in a tent.

Homeless, Gray-bearded, Unaccompanied Minor

Don   August 7th-8th

The next morning we walked from Agno along the west side of the valley that carries the main road and rail links north from Lugano toward the Saint Gotthard Pass. For the next 2½ days, as long as we were following the Ticino River, we expected the walking to be fairly easy. Then things would get a bit tougher as we headed up and over the San Gotthard Pass. Five years before, when I did a week's worth of the Trans-Swiss Trail with my friend Ian (who we'll meet later), we walked half way up to Saint Gotthard from north to south. This time, David and I would be doing it in the other direction.

We walked well up on the western slope and alternated between footpaths and beautiful old towns. In the early afternoon, one of the footpaths suddenly petered out. So much for saving money on maps. David and I argued at length about the route, with me wanting to head west, diagonally across the hill, and David wanting to plough on to the north, scaling cliffs and swinging across ravines on branches like Tarzan. In a brief test of wills, we both started ascending, with me taking the easier route and David taking a diverging route toward a steep rock face. Fortunately, after a few minutes we both capitulated and gradually worked our way to a middle route. For 90 minutes we bushwhacked up steep rocky slopes. I was getting concerned that we would have to spend the night on that mountain – or even worse, backtrack (real men never backtrack!) – when we finally came over the top of a ridge and saw the highway and a town far below. We slid down a ravine, sometimes on our bottoms and sometimes clinging to branches. I was relieved when we finally came to a path that led to a dirt road that joined a paved road that took us to the town.

The valley for about 12 miles above Lake Maggiore is wide (for Switzerland anyway – about 1½ miles at its widest point), flat and fertile. Because it's also on a main thoroughfare, it's relatively densely populated. From the road above the valley we could see a 10-mile stretch of small industrial cities, one after the next. What wasn't city was field after field of greenhouses. As we trudged the final 15 minutes through Cadenazzo toward the campground, we found ourselves walking alongside a 2-mile traffic jam. What a shock to see a backup like that after 6 weeks of mostly tiny villages.

It rained most of the night. In the morning I discovered that one of my boots had fallen over with the opening facing outside of the tent and was pretty wet. Luckily, for the first time in 7 weeks the toilet in the campground had an electric hand dryer. After a half-hour of using it on my boot, I was ready to face the day's hike.

We walked up the valley all morning, following the Ticino River past Bellinzona and Manzanotte to a campground near the small village of Claro. It was beautifully laid out and landscaped like a botanical garden, with exotic plants everywhere. There were hedges every 20 yards or so, and because the ground was on a hill, it had been terraced. That meant that no one in the entire campground was next to more than three or four other people. There could've been 200 people there and we never would have known it.

The clientele of the campground in Claro seemed to be 80% Dutch. When I asked one of them about it, he replied that the ANWB (the Dutch equivalent of the AAA) recommends the place very highly. It's also about a day's drive from the Netherlands, which makes it a good overnight stop for the people heading down to Italy.

In the small activity room we struck up a conversation with a man and his daughter who were from Apeldoorn, which is about 18 miles from where we lived in the Netherlands from 1979 to 1981. I was speaking to them in Dutch, although occasionally, for David's sake, we would switch to English. I'm very proud of my Dutch-speaking ability. While everyone recognizes that I'm not a native, occasionally when I travel in Belgium, someone will think I'm from Holland, and when I'm in Holland they sometimes think I'm Belgian or German. Only rarely will someone immediately recognize me as American. In an attempt to impress David, who is constantly teasing me about my abominable French accent, I asked the man what sort of accent I had when I was speaking Dutch. Without a moment's hesitation, he replied, "Oh, it's certainly an American accent." Rats!

Another man came in and heard us speaking English with American accents and got very excited. He was an American who had been living and teaching university in Amsterdam for 14 years. He seemed pretty desperate to compare notes with another long-term expat, so David and I spoke with him for over half an hour.

No sooner had we put our tents up than it started raining. Earlier in the day, we were lucky enough to take shelter in a bus stop for lunch while a thunderstorm passed over us, but this time the rain meant business. During the afternoon and evening there were 7 hours of thunderstorms interspersed with torrential rains. At one point, one of the stakes of my tent pulled out of the sodden ground, pouring water onto the floor of the tent before I managed to get it fixed. I had to spend most of an hour wiping and wringing, but in the end I managed to contain the damage fairly well.

It continued to pour through the night. Clearly someone didn't want us walking in Switzerland. In an attempt not to anger the spirits, we had stopped any talk about the possibility of the weather clearing up. The few times when it was absolutely necessary to talk about the weather, we would spell. "Do you think it's going to C-L-E-A-R U-P long enough to take off our R-A-I-N G-E-A-R?" It was on that day that I suddenly stopped myself. "Oh, no!" I exclaimed in horror. "Do you suppose God can spell?"

It had now been 7 weeks since we left home, and I was beginning to look pretty rough. I have a blue "kibbutz" style hat that I'd been wearing for my long walks for the past 10 years. It's pretty beat up and I wash it by hand every couple of days, which makes it look even more beat up. With the hat, my unkempt gray beard, my hair getting long, and my ragged hiking clothes (which I'd been wearing every day and occasionally washing by hand for 7 weeks), I knew I looked a lot like a homeless person. Much of the time on the trail I wore a clear map case suspended on a string around my neck to have easy access to the trail maps. The map case looks like what you see unaccompanied minors wearing in airports. So the next time you see a homeless, gray-bearded, unaccompanied minor, be kind to him. There's a chance it may be me.

Blair Swiss

David

I telephoned Angela from the rec room at the campground in Claro, and the conversation started to get a little hot and heavy discussing, among other things, what the dress code should be for our happy reunion. But a group of young Dutch girls kept walking in and out of the room and, unsure just how much English they understood, I kept having to switch conversations in mid-sentence. I suppose there's really no good time for someone to interrupt you when you're in the middle of torrid phone sex.

After a week or two of tooling around in the heat of Italy and not really accomplishing a whole lot, it was real, real nice to be back in the mountains, walking every day and making progress toward a goal, which in this case was to get as close to Zurich as we could before our flight left on the 23rd.

It occurred to me today that this was the most time I'd spent with my father in my entire life. Through my childhood he had traveled extensively for work, and it was rare that he'd spend more than a few weeks at a time in the country before getting shipped off to some other city in Europe 5 days a week. People wondered before we left whether Dad and I would still be on speaking terms by the time we got back. Dad was very concerned about how he and Angela would fare (and, it turned out, with good reason ... "You'd be the perfect weight if you were 6'4"" ... honestly), but not so much about him and me. During this trip we spoke at length about our lives, the way they'd turned out, and what had transpired in the meantime. At one point we talked about my decision to leave my 9-5 job to start my career as a freelance writer – possibly the hardest thing I've ever done in my life, but also one of the best. Dad and I both got a little misty-eyed as he told me how proud he was of me for doing that and for actually making it work. Of course, it could've just been the exhaustion talking.

By now, for the first time since we left, we were starting to develop a rhythm. As we walked hour after hour, day after day, I got used to emptying my brain and daydreaming – about Angela, our future, and our life together; about work, and how I would pick up my business when I got home; coming up with ideas for movies and plays, TV shows and novels and comic books; about winning Oscars and literary awards, selling millions of copies of books and being able to spend my life writing and doing nothing else. Every now and then Dad would say something and I would listen politely, waiting for him to finish so I could return to the daydream I was so thoroughly enjoying.

The first night out of Claro we camped high up on the mountainside in front of an isolated, abandoned house. The house was made of stone and had a barn – also made of stone – which no doubt housed the mule, goat, or other service animal that carried the groceries in from wherever they were purchased when the owners were in residence. It was probably someone's vacation home but could just as easily have been the lair of a psychopathic axe-murdering hermit.

We sat in front of the house for some time, debating whether we should wait, knock on the door, or just pitch our tents expecting/hoping for the best. In the end we opted for the latter, but the only flat spot was directly in front of the house, with the trail running through it. We ate and settled down to rest in our tents while the temperature plummeted. Then, just as it was getting dark, a lone hiker came out of the woods, silently walked between the two tents, and disappeared into the dusk. What the hell was he doing on a mountain trail in the middle of nowhere just before nightfall? Surely, he was waiting nearby in the woods and would be back when we were asleep.

I spent the entire night shivering at the thought that any minute the Blair Witch was going to emerge from the house and drag me inside, kicking and screaming, and chop off my limbs to make soup.

It was a restless night, to say the least, but ultimately we woke up unscathed, as more hikers bisected our camp in the waxing hours of the morning.

The Blair Swiss House

The next day we continued on the trail along the side of the mountain, hoping that the valley would come up to meet us. The altitude of Airolo, the last town on the south side of the Gotthard pass, was only a few hundred yards below where we were camping. After a few miles, though, the trail petered out and we found ourselves walking through dense forest on the side of a cliff, next to a sheer drop of perhaps a thousand feet. I was all for continuing on ahead and taking our chances, but Dad wimped out and insisted that we turn back and then bushwhack up the slope of the mountain until we reached a road. We followed the road uphill for an hour to the tiny hamlet of Gribbio.

This part of Switzerland is filled with tiny villages with small stone houses. Some have cobblestone streets; others, like Gribbio, simply have lush, green grass between the homes. Most of these villages have no grocery store or any other businesses, and many of them are 2-hours' walk from the nearest road. All of Gribbio's cars were parked in a field a few yards away from the houses, in an apparent attempt to make the village car-free. Perhaps they wanted to prevent all the traffic build-ups that would no doubt occur if the two dozen residents were permitted to drive the thirty feet from their front door to the town's single café.

It had been a while since we'd turned heads walking into a place. This was the first time in weeks that we walked into an establishment that catered primarily to locals and not to tourists or passers-by, and as we walked into the café the half-dozen people sitting on the terrace turned and stared at us curiously. We smiled politely and sat down, and they eventually went back to their conversations in a language which we thought might be Romanche but we later found out was a local dialect of Swiss Italian. We noticed with some amusement that more than half of the patrons were wearing Crocs, and that included a 75-year-old man, a 10-year-old girl and, I think, a border collie. The café had five items on the menu: sliced meat, cheese, bread, beer, and ice cream. We had one of each, served by a bubbly young woman named Cosetta (I love that name). We left her all of our Euro change as a tip – we wouldn't need it any more now that we were getting deeper into Switzerland – before heading on.

As we were heading out of town we saw that the trail headed off to the left while the road headed to the right. Both had signs pointing to Dalpe, our next destination. We asked a local which we should take, and he told us in no uncertain terms:

"If you take the road, it's fairly flat the whole way, and it's only a few kilometers. You'll get there in maybe forty-five minutes. If you take the trail, first you'll go *up*. And then you go up, and up, and up some more. And then you go *down*. And down, and down, and down. And it will take you maybe four hours."

Well, since you put it that way. We walked along the road, looking down the whole time on a valley that reminded us of a model village – dozens of different kinds of houses, factories, farms, train tracks and motorways far enough away that they looked just the right scale – before arriving in Dalpe, a much larger town than Gribbio. We spent the night in a hotel (we considered sleeping in a dilapidated, abandoned house, but decided there was too much of a risk we'd be crashing the local teenagers' midnight smoking spot) and in the morning descended to the valley and then followed it to Airolo, the last remaining town before the Gotthard pass. For most of the afternoon we walked alongside the Autostrada, where a 9-mile backup of cars waited to get through the tunnel. We would get a fix on a nearby car or truck and an hour later check to see if we were still next to it. Sometimes it was slightly ahead; sometimes we were.

The Ritual Clothes-washing

Don   **August 11th-14th**

Outside the door of our hotel in Airolo was a post with half a dozen footpath signs. Two of them pointed in different directions to the Hospice of San Gotthard, which is the historic refuge for travelers at the top of the pass. The sign in one direction said 5 hours and 40 minutes and the one in the other direction said 3 hours and 10 minutes. It's not at all uncommon to have multiple footpaths of different lengths and difficulties going to the same place. What is less common is to see both alternatives on the same signpost. A number of times over the past 2 months we'd taken a posted path to our next destination and the path turned out to be longer and harder than we'd anticipated. Later, we found out that another path would have been much shorter and easier.

Before you go with us out of Airolo and head up to the pass, I want to give you some comments on small town post offices and on clothes washing in the camping world. First, post offices. Because I had no idea how much the letters I was writing weighed, mailing them always involved finding a post office. (For that matter, even if the letters were the same number of pages, the postage was rarely the same. Very un-Swisslike!) Nearly every town in Switzerland has a post office, but the smaller the town the more limited the opening hours. Finding a post office that was open in Ticino when we were passing by was getting to be a challenge. On the walk from Claro to Dalpe we passed a post office that was open 3 days a week from 9:00 to 9:45 am and 11:00 to 11:30 am. On the walk from Dalpe to Airolo we passed one that was open from 8:00 to 8:30 am twice a week. For the past several weeks, I had been carrying letters around for 3 or 4 days after they were sealed and ready to go.

Next, clothes washing. Over the previous 8 weeks, clothes washing had become something of a ritual. I use the word "ritual" in the religious sense, as in something that you do for a metaphysical purpose and are not sure whether there is any earthly result likely to ensue.

I had two sets of clothes – convertible hiking pants (with zip-off legs), t-shirts, long-sleeved shirts and socks (two pairs per set: liners and outer socks). Each day's walk, whether hot, cold, rainy or clear, resulted in the clothes that I was wearing being pretty ripe. At the end of each day, I would try to shower or at least wipe myself down, put on the clean set and wash the dirty one. But if we didn't camp early enough for wash to dry on the line, if the weather was not cooperative, or if I was just too tired or lazy, I ended up the next day wearing the clean set and carrying the ripe one. And if that happened for more than one day, then I either had to wear a ripe set for a second day or put on the other ripe set. (So if the gray-bearded, homeless unaccompanied minor that you come across also smells terrible, you'll understand why.) If both sets of clothes needed to be washed, then I had to wear my rain gear during the washing and drying process. This was not a particularly comfortable or fashionable alternative. However, it was better than washing one set and continuing to wear a dirty set, which puts you in a never-to-be-remedied position of always having two dirty sets at the end of the day.

Okay, so why do I classify such an obviously necessary task as a ritual? First, all of the clothes washing that we did was by hand. While it was certainly satisfying to see how muddy the water got while we were sloshing the clothes around, neither David nor I claim to be able to compete with an automatic washer. Second, at least half the time, we had only cold (and I mean ice cold) water. Third, in most of those cases, there was no stopper to the sink, so we had to stop up the drain with a sock and try to soak the clothes before the sock floated away and all the water disappeared down the drain. Fourth, because we didn't want to carry the extra weight, we made do with very small amounts of soap. (That's why the soapy water disappearing down the drain was such a problem.) And fifth, we acquired a lot of stains that weren't going to come out even under ideal washing conditions. For example, 4 weeks earlier in Aigle I got tree sap on the back of one of my t-shirts, and it was still there. I was also on a first name basis with some kind of gummy substance on the seat of one of my pairs of hiking pants.

By this time in the trip we were also having soap availability problems. We'd brought from the U.S. a small amount of a soap called Campsuds, which is designed to be eco-friendly, and tiny amounts of it work splendidly even in ice-cold water. It's intended for washing body, hair, clothes, dishes, and anything else that needs cleaning. We ran out of Campsuds somewhere around Courmayeur and had purchased what we were assured by the clerk at an alternative health products store in Genoa was a reasonable substitute. The problem was that it was the foulest-smelling, most ineffective slop ever created on the planet. Huge quantities of it refused to clean anything, and any time we used it on dishes we would choke for hours waiting for the smell to wear off our hands. With clothes it was even worse; the putrid vapors lasted for days. After a week we threw it all out and bought some liquid dish soap, which we used for everything from then on.

But at least I'd had the sense to bring two sets of clothes and to choose either dark or dirt-colored items. David, against my strenuous objections, brought one pair of convertible pants and one pair of shorts, and had only one long sleeve shirt (a fleece). Both of his t-shirts and all of his sock liners were white. Or rather, they had once been white. By now they'd long since morphed to a grayish-brown – at least those patches of cloth in between the stains.

Nonetheless, in spite of all the handicaps and the apparent futility, we persevered with the daily washing ritual. David complained constantly that, even after washing his dirty socks, they still smelled like dirty socks.

David will now chime in and tell you how his choice of wardrobe was impeccable and that he never had any problem with it. Don't believe him.

(Note from David: Yes, against Dad's strenuous objections I had decided to save some money and buy one pair of convertible pants and one pair of shorts instead of two pairs of convertible pants. In the end, there was exactly once on the entire trip that I would have made use of the extra pant legs if I'd had them, and even then it would have been a convenience, rather than a necessity. By now I was regularly turning to Dad spontaneously and saying, "You know what I really wish I'd done differently? I wish I'd brought an extra pair of pants." Dad didn't appreciate the humor, and I still gloat about the fact that I was right. Oh, and the white t-shirts were

performance-fabric shirts I already owned. I'm not sorry I didn't spend the $100 on two more opaque shirts when I was never again going to use the white ones I already had.)

Who are you going to believe, a 25-year-old bouncy animal who thinks he's going to become an Alphütte Ninja Monk, or a 56-year-old, homeless, gray-bearded unaccompanied minor? I know who I'd go with, but the choice is yours.

The next morning we started up the steep, but well-groomed trail (the shorter one, thank you very much) from Airolo toward the San Gotthard Pass. The weather was glorious – clear with a few scattered clouds and not too hot. The main pass highway, a smaller old highway, and the footpath all had to fit into a valley that gets increasingly narrow as it nears the top. The main highway makes bold sweeping cuts across the valley, often on bridges or through short tunnels. For much of the way there is a roof over the roadway, to protect it from rockslides.

The older road follows the contour of the land more, and makes short "S" curves up the steeper and narrower sections. At one point I looked up and could count 13 switchbacks. Airolo is at 3,870 feet and the pass is at 6,900. We made the ascent in 2 hours and 15 minutes – the footpath sign outside our hotel said that it would take 3 hours and 10 minutes. Weren't we proud? *(Note from David: Yes! We are men!)*

Just below the pass is the San Gotthard Hospice, which for hundreds of years was run by monks as a shelter for travelers. It has recently been restored, and nearby is an old military installation, which is now a museum. In another building are the San Gotthard Pass history museum, a souvenir shop, a cafeteria, and a fancy restaurant. David and I spent an hour in the history museum. Because of a steep gorge that blocked the way, the San Gotthard Pass was not one of the easiest routes from northern to southern Europe until the 12th century. To get around the gorge, travelers had to climb over one of the mountains on the side. In the 12th century, the "Devil's Bridge" (called such because, according to legend, the Devil built it in exchange for the soul of the first one to cross it –

which turned out to be a goat) was built spanning the canyon, and the pass has increased steadily in importance and traffic for the past 900 years. Its history is one of improving roads and bridges and tunnels, and numerous wars over control of the route. The first tunnel, making the pass open year round, was built in the early 1700s. In the 1850s came the railroad, and in 1980 the automobile tunnel. Before the railroad was completed, the stagecoach ran day and night and did the trip from Basel (on the border of Switzerland, Germany and France) to Chiasso (on the Italian border south of Lugano) in 35 hours. Walking it would take around 25 days.

Devil's Bridge

The trail down the north side of the pass was much more gradual than the south side – after climbing 3,000 feet in just over 2 hours that morning, we descended only 1,600 feet in the same amount of time that afternoon. Much of the way down was on the ancient cobblestone mule and cart road – historically inspiring, but hard on the feet and ankles. Shortly after starting down, we began looking for a campsite. We wavered between places in clear view of the road and fields of cows and the resulting omnipresent puddles of cow shit. (Were we even allowed to camp out there? We didn't know.) Eventually, we came across a tiny water-pumping station 150 yards up a small side path. We camped on the side of the station opposite from the road, which was pretty well sheltered by some trees and bushes. Since it was Sunday, we thought it was pretty unlikely that any workmen would come by and tell us to move on.

The next day we followed the valley down through a series of small towns – Hospental, Andermatt, Göschenen and Wassen – to Gurtnellen. They all have nearly as many small hotels and tourist rooms as residents. The arrival of the railroad 150 years ago transformed the economies of these towns from primarily agricultural (with some support of the traffic going by foot and stagecoach over the pass) to quarrying of stone and, because of the large amounts of available water power, to manufacturing of metal. The opening of the automobile tunnel in 1980 transformed them again to more tourist-transit-based economies.

It was starting to rain by the time we reached Gurtnellen, and we were both getting tired after 7 straight days of hiking with packs; so we decided to find a hotel. We found a small, family-run hotel and were once again adopted by the proprietors. Shortly after we settled into our room, our hostess insisted on taking me up the street to show me where the new, more scenic footpath from Gurtnellen down the valley to Amsteg started.

The valley was only a couple of hundred yards wide at that point, with the highway on one side of the hotel and the railroad on the other. Our room overlooked the railroad, and trains came thundering past our open window every 10 minutes or so throughout the night. It didn't make for a particularly restful sleep, but it sure beat the hell out of sleeping out in the rain.

It was an easy if somewhat long walk the next day down from Gurtnellen to Amsteg and then north along the flat Reuss valley to Altdorf. The magnificent scenery was somewhat spoiled by the constant roar of the motorway and the sight of the road and the railway in the narrow valley. In Erstfield, about 4 miles before

Altdorf, we went into a grocery store and bought a loaf of French bread, lox, herb cream cheese, yoghurt, fruit, and a huge bag of paprika-flavored potato chips for lunch. Actually, the whole day was pretty good from a food standpoint. Breakfast in the hotel had been orange juice, two kinds of bread, five kinds of jam, three kinds of meat, six kinds of cheese, and a selection of teas. For dinner that night, we made penne arrabiata with onions and meat sauce. By that time we were getting pretty good at one pot / one burner cooking.

Drama Queen

David   **August 14th-17th**

Altdorf is called "the crossroads of Switzerland," a nickname that seems to be well-deserved. We had come through Altdorf on our westerly journey through Switzerland, and now here we were, 7 weeks later, passing through it on our northbound trip.

We made our way to the tourist information office where I vividly remembered the minx from the first time we visited – a petite young thing with angular facial features and a small stud in her nose. She was there but, much to my disappointment, was occupied with other customers.

We had decided to go to the tourist information office for two reasons – one, force of habit, and two, because Dad wanted to find a campsite that was quieter than the one we'd stayed at the first time, which was next to the main highway that heads through the Gotthard Pass.

Dad began talking to the clerk in German, and when she pointed on the map to the campsite we'd stayed in before, Dad asked if she had any other suggestions – that we'd stayed in that campsite before, and it was right next to the road, and how do you say "noise" in German?

I hadn't had a problem with it, and was annoyed that we were here to begin with so I piped up, saying, "Oh, it wasn't that bad! How do you say, 'drama queen' in German?"

To which Dad turned to me with venom spewing from his eyes and said, "How do you say, 'asshole' in English?"

The clerk giggled nervously, as did I, which served to diffuse some of the tension, although there was no doubting by now that Dad and I had spent enough time in each other's company. We'd gotten into a fight a few days before, the night we camped by the water pumping station. We'd filled our water bottles from a pipe that ran from the mountain stream above the highway into the larger stream below, and as per usual, Dad had insisted on purifying it, even for the water we were using just to do the dishes. For weeks I'd been making fun of Dad for being overcautious in purifying our water after two or three instances of him eating a dropped cracker or nut off the ground – "The floor of a bus stop is sterile, but if it comes from a mountain stream it's poison," I'd say.

Well, by now Dad had had enough of it and verbally bitch-slapped me for not only making fun of him on this topic to his face but doing so behind his back in my conversations to Angela and my e-mails back home. I apologized and resolved not to say anything anymore. Although the floor of that bus stop *was* pretty nasty. *(Note from Don: What David is neglecting to tell you is that 50 yards up from where we were camping there were cattle drinking from the stream, not to mention shitting and pissing in it. Cryptosporidiosis (severe diarrhea and nausea) and giardosis (diarrhea, lactose intolerance, severe joint pain) are what you get from drinking untreated water from mountain streams. They are rarely fatal for healthy adults, but still not a particularly fun way to spend the rest of your summer.) (Response from David: One of the peanuts Dad ate off the ground was in the middle of a field with cows – if the water is deadly, isn't the ground that they're shitting and pissing on deadly, too? Plus, magic mushrooms are grown in cow patties, and I've never gotten cryptosporidiosis or giardosis from those ... .)*

Despite almost launching into a fistfight in the lobby of the tourist information office, we ended up at the same campsite. I was quite looking forward to greeting the hosts we'd met 7 weeks earlier and informing them of our success in crossing Switzerland and all the adventures we'd had since.

We stayed there for 2 nights – we hadn't had a rest day since leaving Agno 9 days earlier, the longest we'd gone without rest in 8 weeks of hiking. Unfortunately our timing was pretty poor – that day was some kind of Ascension Day for Swiss Catholics, so it was a religious holiday in all the Catholic cantons, of which Uri is one.

We'd wanted to spend the day sending e-mails and maybe finding a movie theatre (I majored in film in college, so after 8 weeks was suffering serious cinematic withdrawal), but for the umpteenth time were unable to find a movie theatre that was both open and showing movies in English. Instead we spent the day lazily reading, writing, resting, generally being bored, and watching *Pimp That Ride* with German subtitles on the flat panel TV at the Burger King next to the campground.

In the morning we left Altdorf and headed north along the Urnersee, the southern-most of the lakes that zig-zag up toward Schwyz and Lucerne. According to the legend, when the bailiffs arrested William Tell they took him on the Urnersee, where they met an unexpected storm. Tell was a much more experienced boatsman than the bailiffs who arrested him, so they untied his hands so he could help them navigate the craft through the storm. Tell steered the boat toward shore, jumped off, and then pushed the boat back into the waters, successfully escaping the bailiffs. He began rallying the people of Schwyz, Uri, and Unterwalden (the three territories that came together in that area) to fight the oppressive Hapsburgs. On August 1st, 1291, they assembled on Rütli Meadow and signed the Swiss Federal Charter, uniting as allies what became the first three cantons. They defeated the Hapsburg army in 1315, and have been joined by 22 more cantons in the 7 centuries since.[23]

That morning we walked past the Tellskapel, a rather large chapel built on the spot where Tell is supposed to have jumped off the boat and escaped the bailiffs, on the eastern side of the Urnersee. The chapel has four paintings depicting the "Greatest Hits" of William Tell – refusing to bow to the bailiff's cap; escaping the storm; the baron's bloody death; and the signing of the charter.

Dad and I began thinking what a great video game the whole William Tell story would make – in Level 1 you have to develop your skills as an archer, a boatsman, a warrior, and a diplomat. Make sure your "arrogance" ranking is high too, or else you won't be able to disobey the bailiff's direct order. Then you have to shoot the apple off your son's head. If you shoot the little nipper in the face you lose a life (or your son does, anyway). Then, when you're arrested, you have to steer the boat in the right direction and jump off. Oops, you didn't jump far enough. Blub-blub-blub, you drown. That's another life. And then of course, after killing the baron, you have the diplomatic negotiations phase. You called the President of

---

[23] Unterwalden split in two in the 13th and 14th century, which means there are 26 cantons total. Each canton has its own flag, including our personal favorite, the Glarus Fridli.

Schwyz an incompetent scrotum?   Too bad, negotiations fail, Switzerland isn't a country.[24]

This train of thought kept us going, through the fog, rain and driving mist, all the way into Brunnen, our last campsite of the trip.

---

[24] Check our website for updates on the upcoming release of *Tell Tale: The Video Game*.

Jakobspilger

Don

August 18th-20th

The campground in Brunnen was at the end of a peninsula jutting out into the lake. What a beautiful place! We spent much of the day sitting on the shore watching the ferries go back and forth on their rounds of the towns on the lake. The tourist town of Seelisberg is across the lake from where we were camping, out of sight on top of a plateau. On the shore is a tiny dock where a ferry stops every 20 minutes. Leading up over the edge of the plateau from the dock is a funicular train, and 2 minutes after the ferry pulls away, the funicular starts its slow journey up the hill. Everything works like – well – like a Swiss watch. What else would you expect?

The Urnersee and the Vierwaldstättersee together form what looks on the map like a small flight of steps zigzagging across central Switzerland. Brunnen is at the corner of the first riser and the first step. From our campsite we could look south to Fluellen and up the valley toward the mountains guarding the Gotthard Pass, and west toward the town of Buochs and past it to the mountains of the Berner Oberland. The birds chased each other around the lake near the shore, and occasionally a sailboat came gliding by. To the east stood the magnificent rock faces of the two Mythen peaks above the town of Schwyz, which is the historical center of the canton of Schwyz.

The next morning we walked into town to meet Ian, an Australian former co-worker of mine who lives near Zurich and now teaches at the International Community School there. He had taken the train in from Zurich and was going to walk north with us for the next 2 days. Ian is about 5'4" and in his early sixties. He has a broad forehead that slopes up and back to what little fringe of hair remains after a 40-year career as a mathematician, IT executive and teacher. We had been colleagues for nearly 20 years, initially with me working for him, and years later with him working for me.

From the train station we took a bus about 10 minutes to Schwyz, and an hour later, we boarded one of the three buses a week that heads up to the Ibergeregg Pass. The Ibergeregg bus was full of hikers going to spend the day in the hundreds of square miles of low mountains and high valleys that make up that part of Switzerland. Of course there were lots of footpaths we could have taken to walk up to the high areas. In fact, at the Schwyz bus station there were more footpath direction signs in one place than we had seen yet. But in deference to the fact that Ian was coming with us and was not in shape to climb 3,000 feet and then walk 12½ miles through the mountains, we decided to take the bus the first part of the way. I can assure you that the fact that this would also save David and me from having to climb for 2 hours before starting the 5½-hour walk to Einsiedeln never once entered our minds.

The route we had chosen to Einsiedeln followed a series of ridges joining the tops of a number of low peaks. The next 3½ hours was a series of 20 minutes up and 20 minutes down, along the tops of the ridges, with the terrain dropping on either side of us. Because the terrain was fairly accessible, there were a lot more cows (and cow patties) than we'd had to deal with for the previous couple of weeks. And because of the rains of the last 2 days, the cow patties were mostly cow patty pools. And a lot of what wasn't cow patty pools was mud. Nonetheless, the walk was pleasant and, because the sky was mostly overcast, we stayed cool. Ian and I spent a lot of the day talking about old times, and with the end of the trek looming, David and I were in fine spirits.

As we came over the final peak toward Einsiedeln, I suddenly felt a stinging pain just above my left ankle. The pain quickly intensified, and the skin around the center of the pain started to go numb. At first I thought I had brushed against a nettle, but the trail at this point was clear of underbrush, and I've had enough nettle stings to know that this was something else. I was asking Ian whether there are any poisonous snakes in Switzerland when I reached down to examine my leg. Suddenly, the fourth finger on my left hand got the same pain. Then we saw a wasp on the top of my sock. It must have gotten under the sock and was stinging everything it came into contact with. For the next 40 hours these wasp stings went from sharp pain to numbness to aching and swollen to itching terribly. What a fuss I made. I don't want to seem like a big baby, but – OK, I guess I am a big baby.

Einsiedeln Kloster

For the last 15 minutes or so of the walk we got a fabulous view of Einsiedeln with its huge cloister and its famous cathedral. The cathedral is a pilgrimage destination for tens of thousands of Christians a year, due largely to a black statue of Madonna (the mother of Jesus, not the rock singer). There were hundreds of people walking in and out of the cathedral, and dozens of buses in the parking lot across the street. After taking a quick peek around the cathedral and at the statue, we walked through an outdoor theater that was set up in front of the cathedral for some kind of nightly religious play, and headed for the tourist information office. There I asked the information agent, "Is there a hotel in Einsiedeln that's reasonably inexpensive?" She gave me a bemused look. I continued, "Or, if not reasonably inexpensive, at least not unreasonably expensive?"

She replied, "Here in Einsiedeln, everything is expensive." Then she took a closer look at our backpacks and at my now saintly if somewhat wild looking long gray hair and beard and asked, "Sind Sie Jakobspilger?" ("Are you Jacob's pilgrims?")

I replied that for the past several days we had been walking along the St. Jacob's Pilgrims Path and we would continue to do so for the next day or so, but that we weren't Jacob's pilgrims.

She gave me a sly smile and said pointedly, "You are Jacob's Pilgrims!" She then picked up the phone and dialed a number and told the person at the other end of the line that she had three Jacob's Pilgrims and asked if there were any beds for the night. She got an affirmative answer and booked us a single room and a double room in the Swiss Youth Education Center, a Catholic conference center about a 10-minute walk from the town.

During the walk over, I instructed David to tuck his Jewish Star necklace inside his shirt, and we discussed how we would get away with deceiving a Catholic missionary into thinking we were pilgrims. By now I looked like an apostle, so I could pull it off, but David is a terrible liar. We thought that he should just pretend to be a mute on the off chance they tried to communicate with him in English. In the end we agreed that, while we weren't going to lie if asked a direct question, neither were we going to volunteer any unrequested information.

We arrived at the center, a set of modern brick and concrete buildings, and were greeted warmly at the reception. As we were checking in, the receptionist looked at our backpacks sympathetically. I said, "Yes, we've come from Brunnen today and are going to Pfaffikon tomorrow." Both were true statements, and both towns are on the Jakobsweg.

The woman looked at me quizzically and said, "Most people do the pilgrimage in the other direction." When am I going to learn to stop selling when I've made the sale? For a second I started to panic, but she seemed to have put down our apparent confusion regarding recommended direction of travel to the fact that David and I are Americans and Ian is Australian.

Next she asked if 7:30 am would be OK for breakfast the next morning. I was thinking that I should put a pious look on my face and say, "Yes, I think we can be finished praying by then." David later told me that he was thinking of saying, "But we've got to be in church by 8!" Fortunately, this time we simply said, "Yes."

The rooms were the nicest we'd slept in since Patrick's flat in London 9 weeks before. They had huge, fluffy towels and even bathrobes (!!), although the toilets and showers were still at the other end of the hall. After taking showers and doing some laundry, we walked into town and had a four-course meal with booze and dessert in a Chinese restaurant.

As I've mentioned before, 5 years earlier my father-in-law Richard and I had walked for 60 days from south to north across Britain. Fifty miles from the end of the walk at John O'Groats, we stopped for the night at a bed and breakfast in the Scottish coastal town of Brora. That night just as we were finishing dinner, I started feeling faint. The next thing I knew, I was coming to on the floor, dripping with sweat, and with the sound of an ambulance siren coming up the drive. The ambulance took me to the little clinic in Brora, where a doctor checked me and then sent me on to the nearest hospital, which was in Inverness, 55 miles farther south. At the hospital they did a battery of tests, the results of which were all normal, and kept me overnight for observation.

The next morning, a white-haired old doctor, followed by an overdose of interns, stopped in front of my bed. The doctor discussed my case with the interns for a few minutes. At length, he asked me, "What do you think happened?"

"Well," I answered, "I've walked 18 miles a day for 56 of the last 57 days. I've lost 25 pounds. Yesterday, I walked 23 miles, and had a couple of crackers and some nuts and raisins for lunch. Last night, I had a huge dinner, with wine and dessert. I think that my body decided to send what little blood it has left down to my stomach to process all that food, and forgot to leave enough of it behind to take care of my brain."

The doctor more or less agreed with my diagnosis, and recommended that I take a day's rest, drink lots of fluid, and then go finish our walk. Which is what we did.

Why am I telling you this? Because that night in Einsiedeln, the exact same thing happened. Ian, David and I had just finished dinner and were waiting for the check, when I started to feel dizzy. I turned toward David. "I'm going to pass out now, but don't call an ambulance. I'll be back in a minute or two." And the next thing I remember I was leaning against David, with sweat streaming from every pore in my body. David said that if I hadn't warned him, he would have thought that I'd had a stroke and was going to be a vegetable for the rest of my life.

Twenty minutes later, I was fine, although feeling a bit nervous. Since my return from Europe, I've had a battery of medical tests, all of which have come back normal. I've done some experimenting on my own, and discovered that whatever it is that happens seems to be triggered by eating a large meal in a high-stress environment after not having eaten much for a number of hours. In that situation, ingesting sugar, whether in the form of processed sugar or alcohol, is a sure-fire way to cause me to feel faint or to pass out. It seems to be something called vasovagal syncope, which David thinks sounds like a female complaint, but is actually just a fancy word for recurrent fainting caused by pooling of blood away from the heart.

The next morning we checked out of the conference center and were pleased to have been charged only 38 francs a person. The walk to Pfaffikon, on the south shore of Lake Zurich, was delightful – gently rolling farmland with a few steeper ridges to cross. The weather was cool and clear. It took us only 3 hours until we started the final steep 10-minute descent down to Pfaffikon.

At that point, Ian asked us if we were going to walk on to Germany or if we would like to stay at his flat for the next 3 days until our flights left on Thursday. I don't want to imply that David and I were anxious to stop walking and camping, but it was hours before Ian got his breath back from us hugging him. From Pfaffikon we took the train, tram and bus to Ian's flat in the town of Ebmatingen, which is located on top of a hill about 25 minutes east of downtown Zurich. That night, David and I took the bus to Elena and Tomas's house, where we had dinner and picked up our luggage.

The Hobo & the 17th-Century French Nobleman

Decompressing in Zurich

David   **August 20th-22nd**

The next day I went to the airport to try to pick up an earlier flight home. I'd looked online and there were plenty of seats available on all the flights I'd be taking, and I got to thinking how much fun it would be to surprise Angela by coming home a few days early.

Before we'd started the trip, Dad had called British Airways and been told that, subject to availability, there would be no problem changing the tickets. But at the airport they told me otherwise. When I finally got through to the 800 number (it was an airmiles ticket, so no one at the airport would touch it) they told me that a change was impossible, so I reluctantly trudged back to the apartment to wait out the next few days and try to recover from what Dad dubbed PTDS (Post-Trek Distress Syndrome) and PTVHS (Post-Trek Voracious Hunger Syndrome).

As you might expect, we spent the next 2 days engaged in an eating frenzy. Dad now weighed 153 pounds, a loss of 20 pounds for the trip. His belt, which had been in Elena and Tomas's suitcase for the past 2 months, was now on the tightest hole – 3 inches in from where he'd left it – and it was still loose. I hadn't had much to lose to begin with, but I was down by a few pounds, too. So we were both more than happy to start putting the weight back on by eating everything we could find. The first night we ate with Elena and Tomas, and the second night we took them and Ian out to eat at Mamma Mia's – I finally got to try this famous calzone, which was good, though frankly did not live up to Dad's hype. *(Note from Don: Don't believe him about this either!)* The next 2 nights Dad and I planned and cooked elaborate meals for our three-man "family" – spaghetti Bolognese, salads, pasta salad, garlic bread, wine, chicken, and everything else that didn't come with the prohibitive Swiss tariff on imported meat. One of those nights Ian came home an hour late, which prompted Dad to throw his oven mitts on the ground and say, "Dinner is ruined!" (Not really.)

We worked on the novel. Since it was a suspense thriller, I read as inspiration *Our Man in Havana* from Ian's extensive library. I spent half a day playing video games on Ian's computer to compensate for 2 months without any. I sawed off Wilson's head so I could bring it home, giving one last hurrah to my Swiss-army knife, which we'd made good use of throughout the trip.

On the second day we walked to ICS – the Inter-Community School where I had attended first and second grade. I have one memory from this school: one day we had an in-class assignment that involved writing about food. I was a writer even then, and finished far earlier than anyone else in my class. I went up to show what I'd done to my teacher, and she told me to go back to my seat and keep working on it. "What would you do if there was a famine?" she asked. I should write about that.

I didn't know what a famine was, so she told me to look it up in the dictionary. The dictionary definition was, "When there is little or no food," so I wrote down, "If there was a famine I would go to a restaurant."

When I presented my updated assignment to my teacher, she burst into laughter and read what I'd written aloud to the class. Everyone in the class then burst into laughter, I hid behind the teacher's desk in embarrassment, and then proceeded to go through 18 years of psychotherapy to undo the trauma.

This is all true – everything except the psychotherapy part. I'm still screwed up because of this incident.

Well, when we went to the admissions office and they began cycling through the names of first- and second-grade teachers that have been around since the late 1980s, there was one name, Cutler, that sounded familiar. We went to her classroom, and because she happened to be free, we knocked on the door and went inside.

"Hi," I said. "I went to this school about twenty years ago, and I was looking for my teacher –"

"What's your name?" she asked. I told her, and she said, "Oh, my, you were in my class!" Not only did she remember me, but she remembered everything about me, who my friends were (rattling off names I haven't thought about in 2 decades), and even the naughty word I wrote on the computer for which I was sent to the principal's office. I mentioned the traumatic experience she'd been party to. She apologized for scarring me for life, and I told her I'd long since forgiven her, which is almost true. At length, we said goodbye and I promised to send her a copy of our book when it was finished.

There was one other incident of note from our final few days in Switzerland. One afternoon, Dad and I walked into Ian's living room to discover him doing the Saturday-Sunday *New York Times* crossword puzzle. Dad and I immediately flocked to his side and stood over his shoulder to help him. Ensemble crossword puzzle solving is something of a tradition in the Fried family, and it never occurred to us that other people might prefer to do their crosswords solo. Ian tolerated it for a few minutes, but when Dad grabbed a chair and sat down, Ian looked at both of us and said, "Bugger this, you two do it," and walked away. We felt tremendously guilty. I left immediately with my tail tucked between my legs, but Dad – even though he, too, recognized the error of his ways – couldn't help himself and finished the crossword puzzle anyway.

In the end, we were glad to spend a few days recuperating, taking some light walks to wind our bodies down, and relaxing before taking the trip home.

Actual Route

The Rain Gods Send a Parting Shot

Don   August 23rd-24th

On the day we departed for home, David and I had one last sample of Swiss public transportation efficiency. At 8 am, we left Ian's apartment and walked the 200 yards to the bus stop. Three minutes later the bus arrived and took us the 18-minute ride to the tram stop, where 2 minutes later the tram came and took us the 14 minutes to the central train station, where 7 minutes later the S-bahn left for the 15-minute ride to the airport. Total elapsed time for four different kinds of transportation, including connections – 64 minutes. Now that's what I'm talkin' about.

The remainder of the day was supposed to be flights from Zurich to London, London to Chicago and Chicago to Denver (from Chicago, David would go to Austin), where I would arrive around 11 pm. It didn't quite turn out like that.

Zurich to London was uneventful, although Heathrow pulled its favorite trick of sending us to the furthest possible point in the terminal before putting us on buses to a remote gate. The good news was that we got upgraded to World Traveler Plus; not quite like business or first class, but a hell of a lot better than sitting in cattle-car. I watched three movies. Nothing like making up for lost time after over 2 months virtually without seeing a TV screen.

About 45 minutes before we were supposed to land, the captain came on the loudspeaker and announced that Chicago O'Hare was closed due to a tornado warning and severe thunderstorms. They'd even evacuated the control tower for a while, so they were diverting the plane to Detroit. Once in Detroit, they refueled and immediately took off again. The plan was to circle over Chicago and be first in line to land once the weather moved on and the airport opened again.

After we'd circled over Lake Michigan for about an hour, the pilot announced that O'Hare was still closed, and since union rules allowed the pilots to work only a certain number of hours which had now expired, they were sending us back to Detroit. We left our holding pattern and had just started heading east, when the pilot came on the loudspeaker again and said, "You're not going to believe this, but we've just been cleared for an immediate, direct landing in Chicago." Spontaneous cheers and applause from 400 passengers. It turned out that "immediate, direct" meant landing an hour later and then taxiing another 40 minutes until we got to our gate.

We were supposed to have landed at 3 pm, but by the time we got through passport control and customs it was 9 pm, and any hope of making our connecting flights was long gone. And because of the weather problems, thousands of passengers were swarming all over the airport trying to make alternative arrangements. (At one point we overheard someone say they were #127 on the standby list). We stood in line at the connection counter for another hour, where David was rebooked onto a Continental flight via Houston early the next morning, and I was booked onto an American flight to Des Moines, with a tight connection onto a United flight to Denver the following afternoon. By now every available hotel room within 25 miles was fully booked. But because of the frequent winter weather problems in Chicago, O'Hare is fairly well prepared for unexpected sleepover guests. They had set up hundreds of folding cots with blankets and pillows wherever there was room in the various terminals. David and I joined about 90 people in what looked like a homeless shelter in the baggage claim area of Terminal 2. There were no cots left by the time we got there, but we had our sleeping pads and sleeping bags. Did someone say "camping?" We decided to forego the tents since we didn't think that they'd appreciate our pounding tent stakes into the linoleum floor tiles.

By this time we hadn't eaten for about 12 hours, so we hauled our suitcases over to the O'Hare Hilton, joined the crowds in a sports bar and ordered the last hot food that was served that night – the power went out 15 minutes after we ordered.

It was about 11:30 pm by the time we got settled on our sleeping pads on the baggage claim floor. Every 2 minutes, all night long, loudspeaker announcements would come on: a) welcoming us to Chicago, which is in the Central Time Zone; b) telling us not to leave our baggage unattended at any time; and c) explaining "3:1:1" – you can only get through security with 3-ounce maximum containers of liquids or gels, you have to put them in a 1-quart Ziploc bag, and you can only have one Ziploc bag.

At 4 am, those of us who had managed to get to sleep were awakened, and all the residents of the homeless shelter were told by the police to move along. Apparently, they needed their terminal back.

It occurred to me that, with the tight connection I had between airlines in Des Moines, and given what was going on with tens of thousands of passengers being delayed and rerouted, unless I somehow let United know that I would not be arriving in Des Moines until a few minutes before the plane left, I was sure to get bumped. I walked the mile to the United terminal, where a line of perhaps a hundred people waited at customer service. Fortunately, I'd spent lots of time going through O'Hare, so I knew to walk another 10 minutes to a more remote counter, where there were only about 10 people in the line in front of me.

I had not counted on having to convince the ticket agent that my flight existed. I showed her the documentation that American had given me, which clearly stated that the first leg was on American and the second leg was on United. This woman responded, "This is an American ticket. It has nothing to do with United."

I showed her where it said United for the second leg, so she looked on her computer and informed me, "There's no United flight with that number at that time from Des Moines to Denver."

Normally, my response to this would have been explosive (or at least expletive), especially after what I had been through in the last 36 hours. Amazingly, I was still pretty calm, probably as a result of 9 weeks of life at 2 miles an hour while walking through the mountains. I calmly told her that everyone else seemed certain enough that the flight existed, so I asked her to check it again.

She gave me a look of infinite disdain, checked again, and responded, "Oh yes. Here it is." In the end, she gave me a slip of paper that apparently meant that United recognized the tight connection and wouldn't bump me.

As I waited the several hours for the Des Moines flight, the monitors started listing delays for my flight. Every 10 minutes the departure time would be pushed back by another 10 minutes until the departure time was later than my connecting flight, so I called up Rhonda and asked her to get on the computer and do the heavy lifting, since I was no longer mentally fit to make any decisions. Perhaps I should rent a car and drive from Chicago to Boulder (1,000 miles). I'd probably get home quicker than the airlines could get me there. When I called her back an hour later, she said that American could send me from Des Moines to Dallas, where they could get me on a flight to Denver that landed at 11 pm.

In Des Moines, things suddenly started to go right. The flight from Des Moines to Dallas was early, and in Dallas I managed to get a standby seat on a much earlier flight and arrived in Denver at 8 pm. Rhonda was there to meet me, and after a minimum of searching located my suitcase sitting on the floor in the United baggage claim area where it had been waiting for the last 10 hours. Overall, it had been 45 hours of traveling time, and I arrived 21 hours later than I was supposed to.

The first couple of days back were a strain, to say the least. As expected, I was hungry 24 hours a day. Less expected was the fact that although I was absolutely exhausted, I was managing to sleep only about 4 hours a night. As I write this, 4 months later in mid-December 2007, my sleep is back to normal, but I'm still constantly hungry.

Nonetheless, I'm starting to get some ideas about walking the Colorado Trail, 500 miles from Denver to Durango, next summer. It **never** rains in Colorado in the summertime. Well, maybe sometimes. But I'm used to it.

Burning Up On Re-entry

David

There actually were cots available at the Chicago airport when we first got there, but we decided to give them up to people who didn't have their own sleeping bag as an option. Besides, we wanted to go to the adjoining hotel for dinner, and we didn't think it would be a good idea to use our suitcases to mark our territory – we could just imagine coming back after dinner to find the bomb squad searching through our bags.

In spite of the sleeping bag and ground pad, I didn't get any sleep that night. Angela had taken the day off work to welcome me home, and when I called from Chicago to let her know I wouldn't be coming home till the next day, she was devastated. "It's not fair!" she cried. Indeed, it wasn't fair, and I was devastated, too. I began bitching incessantly about how this wouldn't have happened if I could have gotten on a flight 3 days earlier like they'd said we could. Dad and I got into a fight about something stupid and we walked off in separate directions. It took us half an hour to find each other again and kiss and make up.

When I did finally get home, everything was magical. Angela and I celebrated my return with a trip to Texas Land and Cattle for the ribeye steak I'd been dreaming about for a month. We went to my brother's house, where my 2-year-old niece, who was barely talking when I left, insisted I carry her around for the next 3 hours while she repeated her new favorite phrase, "I'm so happy to see you! I'm so happy to see you!" Every now and then she'd change it up and say, "You're so happy to see me!" Friends and family told me how much they enjoyed getting the e-mails I'd been sending, and they all greeted me with big smiles and warm hugs.

And then things went sour.

I struggled to find a place to live for the 7 months until the wedding. I ended up renting a room in a house with no carpeting and no air conditioning, and since I was never there my cats refused to have anything to do with me. They became best friends with my landlord and hid underneath his bed whenever I'd come home. The only way I could get them out was to crawl on my hands and knees in his bedroom – which would have been bad enough, except that I frequently discovered used condoms or month-old leftover zucchini or would put my hand in spilt massage oil. I moved out a month later, and after bumming a few more weeks in Mom's apartment, came to Colorado to begin working on this book with Dad.

My freelance writing and editing business, for which I'd spent a year and a half building momentum, was now completely inert. It would take months before I even had a few hundred dollars coming in at a time, and with the expense of the trip, I really couldn't afford that. Angela had financial issues, too – which the trip to Europe had compounded – and we ended up breaking off the wedding, in part because I couldn't justify spending $20,000 on a weekend-long party when neither of us could afford to pay our rent. Though Angela and I are continuing our relationship it was a difficult time for all of us. I said a lot of things I regret that put a tremendous strain on my relationships with friends and family. As a result, Angela's best friends now think I'm a sleaze, and to be honest, I can't really blame them.

In the end, Dad was right. I got Post-Trek Distress Syndrome, and I got it bad.

Early on in the trip – after the first week or so – I had started thinking about how much fun it would be to do something like this every year. There's a UT student organization that bicycles from Austin to Anchorage every summer to raise money for cancer – 4,500 miles over 70 days. I've wanted to do that for years. Chile is 2,880 miles of mountains north to south. That could be fun, too. I talked about going on safaris and hang gliding my way across continents. Through all these suggestions, Dad said, "Wait till a few months after this is over, and then tell me how ready you are to do it again."

Now I see what he was talking about. I might do it again a few years down the line, if this sort of thing becomes a career and spending 6 months out of work doesn't cause a huge financial burden. When I'm retired and am looking for a bonding experience with my son or son-in-law, I might do it then. In the meantime, I think I'd be better off pretending I'm a real person and maybe getting a job or something like that.

People still ask me how it was, spending 2 months hiking through the Alps with my Dad. We walked about 500 miles and – not including airplanes – traveled twice that distance on public transportation. We spent 20 nights in hotels, 26 nights in campgrounds, 8 nights camping rough, one night in a barn and one night in the base station of a ski-lift. We ate an estimated 200 peanut-butter-and-jelly-on-crackers sandwiches and roughly 15 lbs of tuna fish.

We endured day after day of rain; and when the rain stopped we endured day after day of thick, muggy heat; we had blisters, sore feet, and aching hips and knees; we slept in the cold, in fields covered in cowshit and with water splashing on our faces; we wore dirty, disgusting clothes and "washed" them by hand, usually with no discernable effect. And after it was all over, re-entry was a nightmare.

But we also crossed Switzerland on foot, and we hiked the Tour de Mont Blanc; we cycled to Montreux and were tongue-napped in Gsteig; we saw avalanches fall from the Jungfrau, and day-in day-out we could see postcard-perfect scenery just by pausing in our tracks and looking up; we ate pounds of local cheese and drank gallons of local beer. And in the end, there's no way I can say I didn't have the time of my life.

All of that doesn't fit into a nice little ball. It doesn't have quite the same ring to it as, "Awesome!" which is the answer people are no doubt expecting. So usually, when they ask me how it was spending 2 months hiking through the Alps with my Dad, I just offer a sly little smile and say simply, "Oh, it had its ups and downs."

Epilogue

As we write this it's October 2008, and we're finally putting the finishing touches on this book before sending it off to print. Angela and David did get married, albeit a few months later than planned, and they're in the process of moving in together and settling down to a life that doesn't include any marathons, triathlons, or extensive trips to the far reaches of the world. Who knows how long it will be before the itch gets them again, but as it turned out, publishing this book was exercise enough.

To Marriage: The Greatest Adventure of All

DaDo Publishing

DA
DO

www.upsanddownsbook.com

Made in the USA